NAME DROP

ALSO BY ROSS MATHEWS

Man Up!: Tales of My Delusional Self-Confidence

NAME DROP

The Really Good
Celebrity Stories I Usually
Only Tell at Happy Hour

Ross Mathews

ATRIA BOOKS

NEW YORK   LONDON   TORONTO   SYDNEY   NEW DELHI

ATRIA
B O O K S

An Imprint of Simon & Schuster, Inc.
1230 Avenue of the Americas
New York, NY 10020

First Atria Books hardcover edition February 2020

ATRIA B O O K S and colophon are trademarks of Simon & Schuster, Inc.

For information about special discounts for bulk purchases, please contact Simon & Schuster Special Sales at 1-866-506-1949 or business@simonandschuster.com.

The Simon & Schuster Speakers Bureau can bring authors to your live event. For more information or to book an event, contact the Simon & Schuster Speakers Bureau at 1-866-248-3049 or visit our website at www.simonspeakers.com.

Interior design by Kyoko Watanabe

Interior illustrations copyright © 2019 by Brad Gibson

Manufactured in the United States of America

1 3 5 7 9 10 8 6 4 2

Library of Congress Cataloging-in-Publication Data has been applied for.

ISBN 978-1-9821-1648-4
ISBN 978-1-9821-1650-7 (ebook)

Dedicated to everyone who never got to sit
at the cool kids' table in the cafeteria.

You can sit at my table anytime. But you
have to share your tater tots.

"Name-Drop" defined:
(verb) The habit of mentioning names of famous people that you "know" in order to make yourself seem more fabulous by association.

"Name-Drop" used in a sentence:
"I, Ross Mathews, would never name-drop. It's tacky. My best friend Gwyneth Paltrow taught me that."

CONTENTS

Contents

PROLOGUE

Name-dropping runs rampant in Hollywood, like high-speed car chases, gluten intolerance, and syphilis. And much like syphilis, name-dropping is super-grody and spreads quickly. You can't walk five feet down Sunset Boulevard without overhearing some Real Housewife of Whatever telling a former Disney tween about how her new trainer is the guy who got Chris Pratt's body into batshit-crazy shape for that comic book movie. No, not that comic book movie. The other one. No, not that one. The other one.

Side note, Chris, if you're reading this—and I just assume you are—I love your body . . . of work. Honey, I'd Guard your Galaxy any day! (Side note: I'd like to point out that I made a conscious choice to not make a cheap, tasteless Uranus joke here. Why? Because I'm trying to be bigger than that. We'll see how long that lasts.)

As someone who has interviewed just about every celebrity you can imagine on every red carpet you can imagine for nearly the past two decades, I have some pretty amazing stories. And, trust me—the red carpet stories are the *boring* ones! The stories where I actually get invited into celebrities' secret lives—their natural habitats, if you will—are the real gold. Their private tables in restaurants, their magnificent movie trailers, their hilariously humongous houses—that's where the really good stuff happens.

From time to time, I've managed to sneak beyond the velvet rope that separates them from us mere mortals and see what few ever get to see.

The following Hollywood stories are wholesome and hilarious. No celebrity was harmed in the making of this book. But don't worry, honey—we're still gonna go there. I mean, don't you wanna know what Kanye piled onto his plate at the buffet when I was in line behind him at the Kardashian Christmas party? And who would it hurt if I told you? *Ham*. It was *ham*. See—now you know and nobody died. Well, the pig did, but you can't blame me for that.

No one ever specifically told me not to tell these stories, but I never do . . . Unless you take me to happy hour and ply me with cheap two-for-one cocktails and appetizers. What can I say? I'm a total whore for a hors d'oeuvre!

The idea for this book hit me as I was hanging out with a fun group of friends—some old friends, some new friends, some old friends who, thanks to Botox, look new. After about four Skinny Margaritas (I was going to have only three, but hello, they're two-for-one!), I told one of these exceptionally juicy stories and noticed my friends, their mouths agape, hanging on my every word. When I finished narrating, one of them said, "You have to put that in a book!" to which I indignantly replied, "I could *never*!"

And then I asked myself the same question I did when I was offered Skinny Margaritas number five and six: "Why not?"

You should also know that, in true Ross Mathews spirit, I've taken the liberty of creating a corresponding cocktail and a related recipe—or "Rossipe," as I call them—for each chapter (why should Martha Stewart have all the fun?). What other book has done that for you, huh? Go open up *Moby-Dick*! There's not a single recipe in there—not even for fish sticks! I know—I was shocked, too! No wonder nobody ever read it!

So here we go. Let's get this soon-to-be-classic piece of literature started! Pretend it's happy hour and you and I are sitting at the bar. I look amazing and, I agree with you, much thinner in person. You look good, too. Maybe it's the candlelight, maybe it's the booze—either way, let's just go with it. Just lean in, keep this all between you and me, and do me a favor? Don't judge me if I name-drop just a little. Thanks. I promise this book will be out of this world. Just like Uranus. *Dammit!*

CHAPTER ONE

The Lady Gaga Story

COCKTAIL

A Star Fruit Martini Is Born

½ fresh star fruit

½ lemon

2 teaspoons simple syrup (equal parts water and sugar, heat
until sugar is dissolved)

1½ ounces vodka

¾ ounces triple sec

Combine peeled star fruit and lemon juice in a martini shaker with
simple syrup and muddle together. Add vodka, Triple Sec, and ice.
Shake and strain into a martini glass.

I PRIDE MYSELF on two things: First, I have the absolute best seven-layer bean dip recipe of all time; and second, I have the absolute best Lady Gaga story of all time. And much like my bean dip, this story has several layers, is very satisfying, and may be a bit too cheesy. Great—now I'm hungry.

I love Gaga. The public knows her very well by now, but when she first burst into the mainstream around 2008, it was like a glamorous alien had landed on Earth and taken over. I've never seen anything like it in my life. In what seemed like thirty seconds, we all went from living in a world where "gaga" was just something a baby said, to literally every person in the world knowing who Lady Gaga was. Like everyone. Like, even my mom.

Gaga really sealed the deal for me when she arrived at the 2011 Grammy Awards red carpet inside a giant intergalactic egg. No yolk—that was when Gaga really came out of her shell. (Sorry—egg jokes always crack me up!) I'll never forget watching as that egg slowly opened and Gaga emerged, dozens of hard-boiled photographers scrambling to get a shot of her.

And don't even get me started on that infamous meat dress she wore to the MTV Video Music Awards. I have no beef with that look! As a gay man who has battled with my weight for my entire life, there's no one who can appreciate low-carb couture more than me.

Little-known fact—that meat dress is currently on display at the Rock and Roll Hall of Fame. Umm, okay . . . Maybe it's in a giant Tupperware container or meat locker or something? Is it beef jerky now? And is it just hanging there on display all alone, or does it come with your choice of sides? "Would you like the

Natalie Cole Slaw, some Tina Turnips, or a heapin' helpin' of Cardi Beans?"

But I digress. Back to Lady Gaga and the day we finally met.

Aside from being Liza Minnelli's best friend or the guy who measures Justin Timberlake's inseam, being a judge on *RuPaul's Drag Race* is the best job in the world. I love all my costars, the amazing queens, and the surprise of which superstar guest judge I'll be sitting next to on the judge's panel in any given week.

I will never forget the first day of taping for Season 9. I sprinted into the *Drag Race* studio, carrying my signature bold-print blazer in a garment bag in one hand and an iced Venti Americano with extra ice, just a splash of nonfat milk, and *exactly* one and a half Splendas in the other.

For some reason, though, things seemed different that day. Was it just me, or was everyone being overly secretive? I couldn't help feel like something was up. Had Ru gone brunette this season? Had they replaced me with Randy Rainbow? Was Shangela back . . . *again*!?

I kept overhearing producers talking in hushed tones, but I couldn't understand what they were saying. They kept repeating something about "LG."

"LG will be on the main stage."

What? LG? The appliance company? Are they a new sponsor?

"LG will be ready in thirty minutes."

Is LG our guest judge? I started thinking of who LG could possibly be. *Everyone's favorite Gilmore Girl, Lauren Graham? That would be cool! Republican Senator Lindsey Graham? Umm . . . I don't think so. Larry the Cable Guy? I know that's a stretch, but . . .*

It never once occurred to me that LG could possibly stand for "Lady Gaga."

It all became clear when the sound person came to mic me for the taping. Let me explain something about "being mic'd." You become very close with the person clipping the tiny microphone to your collar or lapel or Man Spanx. Oftentimes they have to run the cord down your shirt or up your leg to the battery pack/ radio receiver thingy strapped in an even more intimate area. You become very close, very fast.

So, while our sound person, the always warm-handed Kristen, was working her technological magic somewhere between my moobs, she casually said, "Let's put your mic on this side because Lady Gaga will be on your left."

Huh? What?! You could have knocked me over with a feather. Actually, there was no need to knock me over—I had literally already fallen back onto the love seat in my dressing room.

That's right, the actual Lady Gaga was going to be sitting right next to me, little Ross Mathews from Mount Vernon, Washington, at the judge's table! The woman with a million hit songs was giving me "A Million Reasons" to need a diaper. "Bad Romance"? More like shit my pants! Forget "Just Dance," I was trying to just breathe. "Edge of Glory"? Girl, I was on the edge of passing out! It may seem "Shallow" to be so nervous, but hey—I was "Born This Way"! (Okay, I'll try to stop now.)

Needless to say, I tried to keep a "Poker Face" (sorry, I had to!), but failed miserably, smiling maniacally and sweating profusely.

I was nervous for a couple reasons. First, I was about to be face-to-face with Mother Monster herself. Wouldn't you be losing it? And secondly, even though we had never officially met, Gaga and I had briefly experienced one sort of . . . strange interaction.

It was on the red carpet at the 2016 Golden Globes. Remember? That was the year Gaga won her first Golden Globe, for Best Actress in a TV Miniseries for *American Horror Story: Hotel.*

I was covering the red carpet fashion for E! and was positioned on a platform about two stories above the action. The view from up there was amazing—you could see every star's every move, not to mention a bird's-eye view of all the guys' bald spots and the ladies' cleavage.

And then, there she was: Gaga. She took my breath away. I'll never forget how she looked that day: long black velvet custom Versace gown and old Hollywood, Marilyn Monroe–inspired platinum-blond hair. Remember, this was before Gaga was an Oscar-nominated actress. But even back then, though there was no doubt Gaga was already a star, she looked like a different kind of star that day—a movie star. I'll go so far as to say—wait for it—a star was born.

Like the rest of the world, I couldn't help but stare. She had always demanded our attention, but this was a moment in time where something had obviously shifted. The planets had aligned, and now she was a true superstar, having proven that she was not only an amazing singer but had acting chops to boot.

There she was—just about fifty feet below me. Now, a big part of working the red carpet involves a certain amount of "playing it cool." Well, let me tell you, that all went right out the window the moment I saw Gaga that day. I was staring at her. I wasn't even being subtle. I couldn't help it. And then, as if she had felt my laser-like gaze, Lady Gaga turned around, looked up, and locked eyes with me. With purpose. For like a long time. She didn't smile, she didn't frown, she just stared.

I was paralyzed. I had no clue what to do. Should I look away? Should I burst into uncontrollable tears? Should I wave my arms and scream, "LADY GAGA!!! IT'S ME, YOUR NOT-SO-LITTLE LITTLE MONSTER, ROSS MATHEWS!!!"?

But I didn't do any of that. I just maintained eye contact until she was pulled away. I remember thinking, *Did that really just happen? What was that all about?*

I couldn't figure out what her eye contact meant. I thought to myself, *Was she saying hi? Does she know who I am? Did I once make a harmless joke about her on* Chelsea Lately *that pissed her off? Or does she have mixed feelings about the bold forest-green velvet tuxedo jacket I'm wearing? Let's be honest— it's not an easy color to pull off.* I just assumed I'd never find out the meaning.

I was wrong. Back to that day on the set of *RuPaul's Drag Race* . . .

I walked onto the soundstage on High Gaga Alert. *Code Red, honey.* As I rounded every corner, I prepared myself to be Gaga-ready. I would be confident, I told myself. But not overly so. The perfect blend of casual fangirl and respectful colleague. After all, we were basically coworkers now—just a couple of regular Joes trying to make a living, you know? No biggie. Be cool. She's just a normal—

OH, MY GOD, THERE'S LADY FUCKING GAGA!!!!!!!!!!!!

Trust me—keeping your cool when you see a superstar like Lady Gaga in person is impossible. I turned into a cartoon version of myself, with steam coming out of my ears, eyeballs popping out of my head, and tongue unrolling out of my mouth. Category is . . . Roger Rabbit Realness!

Luckily, I don't think she even noticed. She walked onto the set and graciously greeted Ru and my cojudges Michelle Visage and Carson Kressley. Then, in front of everyone—my costars, the crew, her entire glam squad, and the ghosts of my ancestors—Lady Gaga turned to me and said, "Ross, I need to talk to you."

Gaga say what? I gulped.

She continued, "Do you remember seeing me at the Golden Globes?"

Huh? What are the Golden Globes? What is happening? Who am I? I tried to catch up. I mumbled, "Ummm . . . yeah . . ."

Then Lady Gaga proceeded to tell a story I'll never forget. A story for the ages. The greatest story ever told. A story that one day Grandpa Ross will sit in a rocking chair and tell his grandchildren over and over again as they roll their eyes because they're ungrateful little bastards who never have to work a day in their lives, little shits.

Gaga continued, "I was in my hotel room that day, right before I had to go walk the Golden Globes red carpet. I was getting ready and I was so nervous. I mean, I'm just a singer and these people are movie stars. What was I doing there? I was literally . . . trembling." Turning to her glam squad, she said, "You were all there . . ."

They nodded in agreement. I just stood there, unable to blink or think.

She went on. "I was petrified. And then somebody turned on the TV and do you know what I saw?"

I didn't know. *Forensic Files*? That show is always on. That annoying "You're killing me, Larry" mattress commercial? A test of the Emergency Broadcast System? I had no clue. "What was on TV?"

"You." She pointed at me. "You were on TV. And do you know what you said?"

Oh dear God, what did I say? I swear I didn't mean it! Or maybe I did! I don't know what's happening! WHAT IN THE FUCK DID I SAY?!?!?!?

She looked right at me—directly through my eyeballs, past my brain, and deep into my soul.

As the entire room watched and listened, she dramatically paused before continuing. You could hear a pin drop. "You were on TV right there in my hotel room and you said, 'I'm just excited to see Lady Gaga!'"

I remembered saying that and I remembered meaning it. What I didn't really think about that day, even though I was on live TV at the time, was that there was any possibility that she could've seen it.

Gaga went on, "After you said that, I took a moment and took a deep breath." As if to illustrate her point, she actually took a big, deep breath. "And then I exhaled." And she actually did, for the benefit of the story. "And then I said out loud to myself, 'I'm gonna go do this for Ross . . . and for all the other Rosses out there.'"

I had now left my body and was watching the two of us talk from above. Two things struck me: This was a once-in-a-lifetime moment and my hair looked amazing that day. I felt like I was about to burst. Or cry. Or both.

I was almost afraid to bring up our odd Golden Globe eye contact moment, on the off chance it was just in my head, but I couldn't help myself. I really felt the need to either verify the cosmic connection I had felt with her at that moment or risk the possibility that she didn't even remember. I went for it . . . "That's so funny because I remember seeing you there on the red carpet."

"I remember, too," she said quietly.

I knew it!

I went on, "And I remember locking eyes with you, and I don't know, but I felt like you were saying 'hi' or something—"

"No!" she interrupted, pointing her finger in my face.

Really? But I thought I had felt it so strongly. How could I have been so wrong?

She smiled and said, "'I was saying thank you'."

Wow. Just wow. I know it's silly, but sometimes I'm such a superfan of famous people that it seems like "they" live on a different planet than "us," you know? It was so surreal to think that something I had said about Lady Gaga would not only be heard by her, but be something that she needed to hear. The lesson here? You never know who might be listening, so always try to put something good out into the world.

And, as if all that wasn't enough, my new best friend and spiritual guru, Lady Gaga, gave me one final gift. Knowing that I wouldn't be able to keep this monumental tale to myself, she wrapped it all up by saying, "And you can tell everyone I said it!"

So that's exactly what I just did.

Oh, and by the way, if you're anything like me, you've been obsessing over my award-worthy seven-layer bean dip since I mentioned it at the beginning of this chapter. So here you go. You're welcome.

Seven-Layer Bean Dip

2 cans refried beans

1 can mild green chilies

Guacamole (I make my own—lime is key!)

1 container sour cream mixed with ½ pouch of taco seasoning

1 cup grated cheddar cheese

1 can black olives

1 cup fresh pico de gallo

1 cup grated Monterey Jack cheese

Six strips bacon

1 green onion, chopped

½ lime

Mix refried beans with the green chilies and spread in the bottom of your dish. Evenly spread the guacamole on top, then the sour cream mixture on top of that. Then pile the other layers, in this order: cheese (reserving some), black olives, pico de gallo, rest of the cheese. Cook bacon until it's crispy, crumble and sprinkle on top. Finally, add a smidgen of green onion on top and squeeze lime over the whole thing. Serve with beer and tortilla chips.

CHAPTER TWO

The View Story, Part One

COCKTAIL

Barbara Walters Old Fashioned with Extra Bitters

2 ounces bourbon or rye whiskey

4 to 5 dashes of bitters

1 sugar cube

Orange and/or cherry (to garnish)

Combine bourbon/whiskey with bitters, add a few ice cubes, drop in sugar cube (and allow to dissolve), and garnish with your choice of fruit.

ROSSIPE

Barbara Waltermelon Salad

Seedless watermelon

Arugula

Balsamic vinegar

Feta cheese

Salt and pepper, to taste

Mint

Cut a 1-inch thick triangle of watermelon and place on top of a bed of arugula. In a saucepan, pour a quarter cup of balsamic vinegar and heat on low, stirring with a spoon often until it reduces and thickens slightly. Remove from heat. Crumble some feta over your watermelon and then, using the spoon, lightly drizzle over the reduced balsamic vinegar. Salt and pepper to taste. Finely chop mint and sprinkle on top.

IT'S BEEN SAID that you should never meet your heroes because you could be sadly disappointed if they fail to live up to your expectations. And that makes sense. After all, celebrities aren't perfect. But honestly, despite having met just about everybody by the time 2007 rolled around, that had never happened to me. Every celebrity I'd met had been wonderful so far. Maybe I had just been lucky? So many of my idols have not only lived up to, but exceeded, my expectations. But then my luck ran out.

I love Barbara Walters. In fact, I wrote a paper on her in college. I know what you're thinking—*You went to college?*

How dare you.

Undeniably a trailblazer, Barbara is one of the most successful people in the history of television. And she did it at a time when they didn't allow someone like her on television—a woman with a "unique voice."

I can certainly relate to that. I always wanted to be on television, but when I was growing up, they would never allow someone like me on TV—an openly gay man with a unique voice.

But she did it, and she did it better than anyone else ever had. In a male-dominated industry, Barbara never backed down, earning as much money as—if not more than—her male counterparts and carving out an entirely new and original genre of journalism.

Barbara paved the way for every "very special" sit-down celebrity interview you've ever seen. Way before Oprah, Barbara's intimate and often tearful conversations with celebrities and world leaders made viewers feel like a fly on the wall getting the inside scoop. She asked questions no one else asked. I mean, "If you were a tree, what kind of tree would you be?" Come on, that's great stuff!

(For the record, I'd be a weeping willow, mostly because I always sob while watching *Steel Magnolias*. I always burst into tears twice during that movie: Obviously when Julia Roberts—spoiler alert—dies, and before that when she—spoiler alert—cuts all her beautiful hair off. Sorry, honey, but that is not a good look!)

Barbara's impact on every broadcaster who has ever conducted a one-on-one celebrity interview cannot be overstated. And needless to say, as someone who has spent more than his fair share of time on red carpets trying to get something new and fresh out of overexposed stars, Barbara Walters has always been a huge inspiration to me.

So when I finally got the chance to meet her, I dreamed that she would adore me as much as I adored her. I also dreamed as a young boy that Santa would bring me a magical pony that sang like Madonna. Neither of those things happened.

When Barbara and I finally met, the dream that she would truly adore me still seemed like a possibility. I had just completed a show called *Celebrity Fit Club* in which I lost forty pounds by competing in events like kayak races against rapper Da Brat and Screech from *Saved by the Bell* while eating Kristin Chenoweth–sized portions of twigs and berries. The show generated pretty good ratings on VH1, so I hired a fancy Hollywood publicist to see how I could (low-fat) milk it for everything it was worth.

I'll never forget when I got the call. "Ross," my publicist said, "you'll never believe it. They want you to be a guest on *The View*!"

OMG. *The View*. I couldn't even. I had watched *The View* every single morning since the show debuted with the OG co-hosts Barbara, Meredith Vieira, Joy Behar, Star Jones, and Debbie Matenopoulos. Despite a few personnel shake-ups throughout the years, the show was still going strong. Actually, it had never been hotter. A little context . . . This was right after my friend Rosie O'Donnell had dramatically left the show as a cohost—for the first time—after that infamous, live, on-air fight with Elisabeth Hasselbeck. It was epic and it was everywhere and everyone who was anyone was now watching *The View*.

I couldn't wait to go on there and discuss those (soon-to-be-regained) forty pounds I lost on *Fit Club*. I remember every minor detail—what I wore (a slimming black tuxedo shirt under a gray blazer that I got at Macy's for an extra 40 percent off the sale price), what I had for breakfast (a turkey sausage breakfast burrito from room service), and I remember what scared me most (how in the hell to be a guest on a talk show).

I'd started as Ross the Intern in 2001, working as a correspondent on *The Tonight Show*, doing everything from covering the Academy Awards, jumping out of an airplane, competing in a demolition derby, and so much more. But, up until that point, I had never actually been a guest on a talk show. How did it work? Think about it—on *The View* at that time there were not one, but three hosts—Barbara, Joy, and Elisabeth. When one of them asked me a question, did I answer just that host or all of them or did I look at the audience? What if they asked me a question I didn't have an answer to? Would there be math involved? And—worst of all—what if I wasn't funny?

Well, it turns out I didn't need to worry. Like Tom Brady with a football or *Liza with a Z*, when it came to talk shows, I was a natural. Not to toot my own tooter (honey, if I could I'd never leave the house), but I killed it. For reals. That segment was the best four minutes of my life. Even better than that one time I had sex! Every joke landed, my banter with the ladies was top notch, and I could tell I was charming the Chanel pants off my journalistic idol, Barbara Walters.

I was on cloud nine, until Miss Walters sent me to a level I didn't even realize existed: cloud ten! After my segment was over, while walking down the hallway backstage, I heard the show returning from the commercial break, and Barbara, still on stage with the other women, saying on air, "We're all still laughing! I think we should have Ross come back and cohost one day, don't you?" The audience burst into applause with agreement.

Ummmm . . . what? *Did Barbara Walters just say on national TV—on a show that I watch every morning—that she wanted more of me?* I couldn't believe that I actually lived in a world where the legendary Barbara Walters even knew who I was. And now she loved and adored me? Somebody, pinch me!

The producers asked me if I could come back in a month to cohost and I answered way too quickly, like I had just been asked out on a date by Ashton Kutcher (arguably in his prime in 2007, although I'd still hit it).

I went back to LA and my normal life, except nothing was normal. I wasn't just Ross Mathews anymore. I was a person who got to go on *The View* and have Barbara Walters as a mentor and best friend. It was a dream story come true. Now when I'd watch *The View* from home, I'd study what the other cohosts did. No detail was lost on me, like how often they chimed in and even how they held their limited-edition, cohosts-only coffee mug. I wondered, *What's in those mugs? Will I get one of those mugs?* (I did. I gave it to my mom. She broke it, bless her clumsy heart.)

Right before this big fruit was to return to the Big Apple for his big break, I went on a big weeklong cruise. Rosie O'Donnell and her then-wife Kelli owned R Family Vacations and asked me to come entertain the guests on board. Honey, I was born to cruise! Bonding with strangers at all-you-can-eat buffets and drunken piano bars? Sign me up!

As much as I love cruises and was ready to have an out-of-control, wild week of shellfish, show tunes, and shuffleboard, all I could think of was my triumphant return to *The View* when we got back to dry land. As we set sail, the Rosie-leaving-*The-View* scandal was still making waves, and Rosie found herself in the eye of the storm *and* the eye of the tabloids. I was so excited and wanted to talk to somebody about it, but I didn't want to rock the boat by bringing it up to Rosie, seeing as how she had just recently jumped ship herself. But one night in her suite on the cruise liner, the always-intuitive Rosie threw me a life preserver in the form of a "What's up, kid?"

"I don't want to bother you with this, but I'm actually gonna guest cohost *The View* when we get back to New York," I told her, a little worried as to how she might react.

I should have known better. She immediately burst into laughter. "That's awesome! You'll be great!"

Relieved, I confessed, "I'm honestly a little nervous."

Rosie leaned forward, looked me right in the eye, and then gave me the kind of guidance and wisdom she's offered since the very first day I met her. "Look, you're very good at being you, Ross. So just do that and you'll be fine."

Leave it to Rosie. She's always been a source of guidance for me. I felt so much better, and the rest of the cruise was smooth sailing. (I promise that's the last cruise pun from this seaman.)

When I got back to New York I met up with my *Tonight Show* crew, who had flown all the way from Burbank to cover my big day at *The View*. They were all so proud and happy for me. These were the same people I'd been working with since my very first segment for Jay Leno, headed by my writer, Anthony. The plan was that they'd film everything I did as I prepped backstage for my big shot at cohosting *The View*, and we'd show it all on air on an upcoming episode of *The Tonight Show*.

Although they are all fun, some segments on *The Tonight Show* are admittedly more work than others. But this one was turning out to be a blast. The crew and I ran around backstage getting away with as much as we could, genuinely just excited to be there. I was then told it was time for me to join *The View* preshow morning production meeting and, unfortunately, cameras were not allowed to attend—only *The View* producers and hosts were allowed. My *Tonight Show* crew wished me luck as I walked—alone—into the lion's den.

I entered the room to find the ladies of *The View* having their hair and makeup done, and I immediately understood why cameras weren't allowed. Not throwing shade! Makeup rooms are sacred places where stars are free to let their hair down, literally. No one wants to look up and see cameras before a hair-don't is professionally transformed into a hair-do. As a natural beauty myself, I don't personally understand, but I try to be empathetic.

There were four makeup chairs, one for each cohost. Elisabeth was in the far corner, Joy was next to her, followed by an empty chair, and then Barbara. I sat in the empty chair between Joy and Barbara and took deep breaths, trying to lower my heart rate and control my flop sweat. To them, this was just another morning. But to me, it was as if I had won some sort of lottery and the prize was the chance to crawl inside my television. The producers all sat behind us as the hosts were getting their makeup done, looking forward into the mirror as they talked to the reflection of the producers behind them.

I was in awe. I was in the belly of the beast—and there were beastly butterflies in my belly! I was seeing what most normal people never get to see and it was fascinating. I kept sneaking a look into the mirror, trying to catch the eye of my new BFF, Barbara. We hadn't seen each other since the last time I was on the show, when I knocked it out of the park and she invited me back in front of everyone live on TV. Remember that? I couldn't wait to say hi and continue our blossoming lovefest.

Here's some insight into how *The View* works. The morning meeting in the makeup room is where they decide which stories they'll discuss on the show that day. The cohosts and producers are presented with a stack of papers with about fifty different story options on them. Then they all discuss who has a good take on a story, which story is the most interesting, and, most importantly, are there any stories they have passionate, disagreeing views on (those always get chosen because the conversations are better when the hosts have opposing opinions).

I was feeling pretty comfortable at this point (or at least I was doing an okay job of faking it), so when they brought up one particular story that piqued my interest, I enthusiastically spoke up. "You know, I have a good take on that!"

The producers all nodded. "Good," one of them said. "Then we should do that one."

Then my friend Barbara, who up to this point hadn't chimed in, finally broke her silence. Needless to say, it wasn't what I was expecting. "Who is he and why is he here?"

The room fell silent. I looked around. Who was she talking about? It suddenly became painfully clear that she was talking about me. I assumed she was kidding. I mean, hellooooo—she had invited me. So I thought I'd respond playfully.

I sang out, way too loud and way too long, waving my arms in the air, channeling my inner Oprah introducing John Travolta, "I'm here to cohost *The Viewwwwww*!!!!!!"

Her face didn't change. Everything was happening in slow motion. Elisabeth—who was so sweet to me—tried to help by reminding Barbara, "Ross was on as a guest a few weeks ago and you asked him back to cohost."

Barbara interrupted her, barking loudly, "Can someone please tell me who he is so I can talk about him on television?"

All the blood drained from my head. I couldn't think. I instinctively knew to remain quiet, but I couldn't help it and the words just poured out of me. Like a wounded child, I looked at Barbara in the mirror and without thinking asked, "Why are you being so rude to me?"

Finally, Barbara turned from the mirror and looked me directly in the eye. "Because I have no idea who you are or why you're here."

Beeeeeeeeeeeeeeeeep . . . CLEAR! Flatline. Dead on arrival.

Listen, I get it. Barbara Walters was much busier than I was famous, and I understood where I ranked in the Hollywood hierarchy—somewhere just below Flo from the Progressive commercials and slightly above Angelina Jolie's creepy brother. So I wasn't insulted by the fact that she had clearly forgotten ever meeting me. But, to be completely honest, I was a little disappointed by her demeanor.

I decided not to take it personally, trying desperately to remain optimistic. Maybe she was just having a bad day? Maybe she had too much on her plate? Whatever the reason, I can assure you of this: Barbara wasn't just some confused older woman. Remember, this was in 2007, and Barbara—even at the age of seventy-seven—was at the top of her game hosting and executive-producing the most successful daily talk show on TV. At the time, she was sharp as a tack and totally in charge.

The producers took mercy on me and kindly wrapped the meeting up quickly. I remained there seated awkwardly, completely shell-shocked. Joy noticed and whispered to me, "Don't worry about her, honey."

When I walked out of the makeup room, my *Tonight Show* crew was waiting for me—cameras rolling—with eager faces, wanting to capture my continued excitement. I shook my head, covered the camera lens with my hands, and mouthed, "No, no, no . . ." while ushering them out of the danger zone and into the sanctuary of my dressing room.

"You will not fucking believe what just happened," I whispered.

I filled them all in and we just sort of stared at each other. "Well," my writer Anthony said, "we've still got to get a good piece out of this, so . . . good luck with that!"

Looking back, it's hilarious. In that moment, it wasn't.

There are times in your life when you have to dig deep and do something that scares the shit out of you. That moment right before you skydive, when you try sushi for the first time, or when you're the only boy at your junior high school cheerleading tryouts—you know what I'm talking about, right? Well, this was one of those moments.

Sure, I could've backed out. Explosive diarrhea is always a good excuse! I could've used that . . . again. But I didn't. I decided to stare fear in the face, and that face belonged to Barbara Walters.

I gave myself a little pep talk. *Just go out there and do what you do,* I thought. *Remember what Rosie told you on the cruise. Be funny. Be real. Don't let anyone get you down.* Plus, maybe Barbara was just having a bad morning and now that she's fully caffeinated, she'll totally change her tune! *Yeah! Everything is gonna be just fine!*

I've always been an optimist. For me, the mimosa is always half-full.

So there I was backstage, all dressed up and with just a touch of powder on my face (like I told you, I really am a natural beauty). My notes were all organized, printed neatly on three-by-five index cards with *The View* logo on the back. Very cool. We were just about to walk out onto the iconic set, sit at the famous *View* table, and entertain a nation. My *Tonight Show* camera was rolling on me as an announcer's voice came on the overhead speaker and said, "We're live in ten, nine, eight . . ."

I felt a mix of terror and excitement, much like I imagine astronauts must feel as they're counted down and thrust into the great unknown.

I noticed Barbara standing right next to me. She looked gorgeous—like the star that she was. Her coif was perfect—not a hair out of place. Her makeup flawless. She looked much more pleasant than she had about an hour ago in the makeup room when she crushed my young dreams. It occurred to me that this was my last chance to get Barbara on my side before we went out on stage and were on live TV together. Maybe, just maybe, if I could get her to understand that I was just a scared kid who had always looked up to her, her hardened exterior would soften and everything would be okay.

The voice overhead continued, ". . . seven, six, five . . ."

I gulped, took a breath and—with *Tonight Show* cameras rolling—asked, "Barbara? Do you have any last-minute advice for me?"

Without missing a beat, Barbara—my idol, the woman about whom I had written an essay in college—looked me dead in the eye and said, "I'd like to tell you to go out there and be yourself, but I hope you won't."

". . . four, three, two, one . . . And we're live!"

She really said that. And do you know how I know she said that? Because my *Tonight Show* cameras were rolling and, about a week later, we aired it on our show. Our entire studio audience gasped when she said that to me. I even got an apology letter afterward—not from Barbara, but from a higher-up at *The View*. True story.

But back to that moment . . . Right after Barbara offered that oh-so-helpful nugget of sage advice, someone or something from behind me—maybe God or the ghost of Judy Garland?—shoved me out onto that stage and I sort of just went into autopilot. Then, I heard the crowd cheering and saw audience members holding signs with my name written on them and my confidence started to kick in a bit. "Thank you!" I gratefully shouted to the screaming audience.

When Barbara heard me say thank you, she shot me a look and, loudly and in front of everyone, asked, "You think this is all for you?"

What was her fucking problem?!? I mean, no, not all of the applause was for me. But maybe like two of the claps? I'll take it. So I decided to give them a show. I tried to chime in on each topic, I made Joy laugh, and I didn't let Barbara rattle me. And you know what? It went . . . okay. I survived. It won't go down as one of the finest hours in television history, but nobody could tell what had just gone on backstage, so I considered it a success. And it was a great lesson for me to learn as a performer: The audience doesn't care if you've had a bad day, or you woke up with a cold, or an icon that you've always looked up to let you down seconds before you walked out on stage. They just want a good show. And, looking back, it dawns on me now that this could be why I never, ever get flustered anymore. I can handle anything that's thrown my way. So, thanks for that, Babs. I learned a lot from you.

Seems like that should be the end of my *View* story, right? It wrapped up pretty nicely, huh? Well, just like when I assumed

Barbara Walters and I were gonna end up being lifelong friends, you'd be wrong. There's more to this story.

After my less-than-ideal cohosting experience, the worst part of it all was that I could no longer enjoy watching *The View* with my morning cup of coffee. It's like when you eat too much ice cream and it makes you sick—so sick that you can't even look at ice cream anymore (I'm happy to announce that ice cream and I have since mended our relationship). But, for the longest time, that's how I felt about *The View*. I guess you could say I had a form of PTSD: Post-Talk Show Disorder. Just hearing the theme song to *The View* would make my left eye twitch. And the sound of Barbara's voice? "I'm down here . . . under the bed."

So fast-forward nearly a decade. It was 2014. Back then, Hillary Clinton was already laying the groundwork to become the very first female president of the United States. And, believe it or not, I very nearly became the first male permanent cohost on *The View*. Well, we all know how things turned out for Hillary. The truth is, it didn't go much better for me . . .

CHAPTER THREE

The View Story, Part Two

COCKTAIL

Whiskey Sour Grapes

1½ ounces bourbon

¾ ounce fresh lemon juice

¾ ounce simple syrup (equal parts water and sugar, heat until
sugar is dissolved)

Grapes

Combine bourbon, fresh lemon juice, and simple syrup. Pour over
ice that is, like my dreams, crushed. Garnish with frozen grapes.

PB & Jealous Crumbled Dream Bars

FILLING

- 1 pint fresh raspberries
- 1 pint fresh blueberries
- 1 pint fresh blackberries
- ½ cup sugar
- 1 tablespoon flour
- 1 tablespoon cornstarch
- 1 lemon

CRUMBLE

- 3 cups rolled oats
- 3 cups flour
- 2 cups brown sugar
- 1 teaspoon baking powder
- 1½ cups melted butter
- ½ teaspoon salt

ALSO

- ½ cup peanut butter chips

DIRECTIONS

Wash berries and allow to dry. Mix with sugar, flour, and cornstarch, as well as the juice and zest of one whole lemon.

In a separate bowl, mix oats, flour, sugar, baking powder, and butter. Mix until it has a "crumble-like" texture (don't overmix). Place parchment paper into a 9 x 3 baking pan. Gently press ⅔ of mixture (we save the rest for the topping) into the bottom of the pan and bake for 10 minutes at 350°.

Take out of the oven, spread berry mixture over crust, sprinkle the remainder of the crumble mixture over, and then evenly disperse peanut butter chips on top. Bake at 325° for 25–30 minutes. Remove from oven, allow to cool, and cut into bars.

THE VIEW IS notorious for shuffling cohosts more often than a Las Vegas dealer shuffles cards. And let's call a spade a spade—they really go through them. I dare you right now to try to name every person they've ever hired, fired, or rehired. Good luck with that. I just googled it: twenty-one. Blackjack! By the time this book is printed, who knows what that number will be? And back in 2014, the producers were on the lookout to shake things up like they'd never been shaken before. But of course, I assumed for me, it just wasn't in the cards.

The View cohosts at the time were Whoopi Goldberg, Sherri Shepherd, and Jenny McCarthy, with Barbara still making the occasional appearance. The show was headed in a different direction—rather than showcasing the heated political debates they'd become so famous for, the producers were now trying to make the show more light, fun, and spontaneous—like me at my goal weight. As a viewer, I welcomed the change. Let's be honest—it's hard to enjoy your morning coffee and breakfast of cold leftover pizza (what was that about my goal weight?) while four passionate and opinionated people scream at each other about everything from water births to waterboarding.

Whatever the reasons, the producers were intent on changing up the show, and making it less argumentative was just the start. Unbeknownst to me, they also seemed open to the possibility of adding a cohost who had something none of the prior ladies of *The View* had . . . a penis!

After my disastrous debut several years before, I'd never returned to the show. Or, I should say, I'd never been asked to return. I just assumed I was on some sort of *View* blacklist. Sometimes I'd happen upon the show while flipping through channels and pause to imagine my picture taped to the wall near the security desk with the printed warning, "DO NOT ALLOW! ANNOYING! GETS ON MS. WALTERS'S VERY LAST NERVE!"

I had heard rumblings in the industry that they were looking for new cohosts, but I never dared to dream they'd consider me. For starters, even though she was only doing the show part-time now, Barbara was still in charge. And secondly, I just assumed they were searching for another strong female voice (feel free to insert your own joke about my voice here).

So imagine my shock when my publicist called to tell me that they wanted me to come back to cohost for a day. "You're kidding me," I told her. "I haven't been back to *The View* for more than seven years. Are you sure they mean me?"

She was sure. I admit, I hesitated. Would Barbara be there that day? Did I want to go through all that a second time? I escaped mostly unscathed all those years ago and was grateful for the experience, but it's like a dog who bit you once—do you dare try to pet it again?

But I agreed to do it. I couldn't help myself. I watched the show enough to know that Barbara was only there a day or two a week, so chances were I wouldn't even see her. Plus, I knew they weren't interested in me auditioning for the job, so I thought it would be fun to meet Whoopi Goldberg for the first time (and try to convince her to make *Sister Act 3: Making a Habit of the Habit*, an idea I still stand behind) and hang out with my friends Sherri Shepherd and Jenny McCarthy.

I'd been a fan of Jenny since her MTV *Singled Out* days and got to know her through Chelsea Handler. They were friends, and she was around a lot during the early days of *Chelsea Lately*. She was always so sweet to me and still is whenever I see her.

Sherri was actually one of the kindest celebrities I'd ever met. When she'd gotten the gig on *The View* a few years earlier, she came on *The Tonight Show* to promote it. I ran into her in the hallway and congratulated her. It turns out she had been watching back in 2007 when Barbara was rude to me, and when she saw me she grabbed my hand and said, "I was watching when you cohosted *The View*. I wish they had been nicer to you."

I'll never forget that and I'll always love her for it. (Side note: I love Sherri even more now, because when my mom was diagnosed with breast cancer in 2018 and was losing her hair due to intense chemotherapy, she sent her—a woman she'd never met—a big box of beautiful wigs from the Sherri Shepherd Wig Collection. Sherri is the real deal. A "big wig" with an even bigger heart.)

This time at *The View*, there was less stress. What was the big deal? After all, I'd already cohosted before and—let's be honest—it couldn't possibly go any worse than that time, so I decided to just have fun with it. My only concern was running into Barbara. Our last interaction still stung, and I'd been dreading seeing her ever since. Luckily we hung in different circles—she was in the upper echelon of the Upper East Side social circle, and I was browsing the ends of the aisles at Target looking for clearance items with the red stickers.

Television studios, much like most television stars, are never as glamorous backstage as they are on camera. Most hallways of TV studios resemble local senior center multipurpose rooms—beige walls, worn gray carpet, scraped-up doors with the paint wearing off around the doorknob. The old *View* studios were no different. I remember walking into the building that day and being overcome with the familiar stale smell and blank walls, except for a few pictures of current and former *View* cohosts throughout the years.

Chills.

Someone important-looking with a headset and a clipboard approached me and said, "Okay, Ross, I'm gonna bring you to the makeup room now so the producers can prep you and Whoopi, Sherri, Jenny, and Barbara."

Excuse me? Beg your pardon? What the hell? Barbara was here? Oh shit.

It was the moment I'd been dreading for years. For the first time I was about to be face-to-face with the only woman who had ever broken my heart. I'd had countless daydreams about how this might go down one day, and each scenario was different, but always dramatic. In some fantasies, I'd confront her directly, bravely holding back tears as I waved my fat finger in her face and really gave her what for. In other daydreams I played it cool, opting to totally ignore her and pretend like I didn't even remember the fact that seven years, three months, and thirty-three minutes earlier she had crushed my youthful spirit.

But in the end, our fateful face-off fell flat. I walked into the makeup room prepared for battle, but instead found a smiling, upbeat, bright-eyed Barbara who extended her hand and politely chirped, "Hello! I'm Barbara. Great to meet you!"

Good move, Walters. Good move . . .

But in reality, this wasn't some sort of move at all. She wasn't putting on an act. She really didn't remember that we had ever even met. Realizing this was a huge epiphany for me. It suddenly occurred to me in that moment that what had gone down all those years ago may have felt like a monumental, epic diss. But for Barbara it was just a Wednesday—just another day of work during a decades-long career that she just had to get through. *Wow*, I thought. *Of course.* Any hard feelings I had been holding on to instantly disappeared.

I shook her hand. "I'm Ross Mathews. We've actually met before. I'm thrilled to be back."

"Well," she smiled, "we're thrilled to have you." And you know what? I think she actually meant it.

That day cohosting could not have gone more differently from the first time. Barbara was funny. She thought I was funny. Whoopi was kind, generous, and everything you'd imagine she would be. My friends Sherri and Jenny made sure I had time to shine, asking my opinion and laughing at my jokes. It was an absolute blast.

As I was packing up my dressing room, filling my luggage with all the uneaten bags of Chex Mix and unopened sugar-free gum from the snack bin, the producers came in and asked if I could cohost again the next day. I looked at my phone, pretending to check my schedule while simultaneously trying not to scream, "YES! YES!! YES!!!"

"Ummm . . . I think I could squeeze that in."

The next day went even better. I was so happy. It seemed that the producers were happy, too. In fact, they kept asking me back, again and again. Week after week, they flew me (first class!) from Los Angeles to New York to cohost the show. I was thrilled to have the work and exposure, but I was mostly just happy to be doing what I loved. I'd dreamt of hosting a talk show since I was just a little kid growing up in a small farm town and, even if I was just a guest cohost, it was happening!

And, at the risk of gloating, I was getting pretty good at it. Each time I guest cohosted, the producers would give me more responsibility. "Let Ross toss out to commercial after the interview in the C-Block," they'd say.

I remember one time I got to introduce a segment where singer Sam Smith performed. We had rehearsed how the other cohosts would come into the frame after his song. It had been staged in a specific way so that the cameras could get the right angle. When one of the cohosts entered on the wrong side, I noticed and quickly maneuvered around her so the cameras wouldn't be blocked, and tossed out to break. "Our thanks to Sam Smith!" I read from the teleprompter. "We'll be right back!"

After that episode, executive producer Bill Geddie pulled me aside. "I saw how you handled that. Live TV is tough and you're a very good broadcaster. Keep it up."

I was thrilled. That's all I needed to hear. I could now die happy.

In a three-week period, I had guest cohosted about ten times, and just like the more you wear your Juicy Couture velour sweat suit, it got more and more comfortable. I was having so much fun, but I knew it would eventually come to an end when they finally hired somebody full-time. Yes, I knew the clock was about to strike midnight and this princess was gonna have to limp back to LA wearing just one tacky glass slipper. (I've never understood glass slippers. How impractical. You know they would *never* get an offer on *Shark Tank*.)

Then one morning, as the makeup artist was putting the final touches on me, she said, "I hope they hire you."

I started laughing. "Honey, you're crazy. They're not gonna hire me."

She stepped back, looking at me. "Why do you think they've had you here so much? They're testing you. I heard them talking about it. They like you a lot."

If you ever want to know what's really going on behind the scenes of a TV show, talk to the makeup department. They know all the tea and the shade, and I'm not talking about T-Zones and eye shadow.

I know it sounds naive, but the thought that I was seriously in contention for the job honestly hadn't occurred to me.

Later that day, after another great show, I was in a rush to head to the airport for my flight to San Francisco, where I was honored to be the grand marshal for that year's LGBTQ Pride Parade, when a senior producer came into my dressing room.

"Listen," she said, sitting on the couch, "we have a big meeting with the executives at ABC this afternoon. Whoopi, Jenny, Sherri, Bill [Geddie], and I have already talked and we want you. We're gonna tell the network that this afternoon. So go home, don't take any other jobs, and get ready to move to New York, okay?"

Start spreadin' the news . . . I'm leavin' today . . . I want to be a part of it . . . New York, New York . . . The whole drive to the airport, I could hear Liza belting out her classic song "New York, New York."

Sing it with me! *I'll make a brand-new start of it, in old New York . . .*

I couldn't believe it. My dreams were all coming true. I pictured myself living as a sophisticated New Yorker. My apartment would be small, but ever-so-tasteful. Would I be a Carrie or a Samantha? Oh, cut the crap—you know I'm a Charlotte. I'd maintain my friendships in Los Angeles, of course, but I'd meet a whole new group of fabulous East Coast socialites to rub elbows with. I'd finally become bi! Bicoastal!

Oh! And I didn't even think about the money! I didn't even know what an official cohost on *The View* made, but I was certain it was more than I'd ever made. I was about to be a rich New Yorker, just like Donald Trump himself, only with better hair and without a solid gold toilet. How exciting!

After a quick nap on the plane, I even splurged for the WiFi, just like a real rich person. Why not? I could afford it now! And just like anyone else would do, the first website I checked online was TMZ. Darling, a talk show host like yours truly simply must be in the know at all times! When the website loaded, I couldn't believe what the headline read.

"*THE VIEW* FIRING MASSACRE."

It was the top story, including a picture of Whoopi, Barbara, Sherri, and Jenny with big red Xs over Jenny and Sherri's faces. I read on, the glass of first-class champagne shaking in my hand.

"*The View* is cleaning house," the article continued. "Network sources tell us the cast has been fired . . . except for Whoopi Goldberg. Our sources say there was a meeting at ABC late this afternoon and they announced Sherri Shepherd and Jenny McCarthy were out. Sources tell us executive producer Bill Geddie also will not be coming back."

That was it—virtually every person in my corner was now out on their ass. The dream was gone and the nightmare was real. It had all gone away, in the blink of an eye. And I found out alone, thirty thousand feet up in the air. I couldn't have been closer to heaven, but I suddenly felt like hell. I had never really had it, that job, but for a few precious hours I'd thought I did, and I really, really wanted it. My heart broke a little on that plane that day.

But what can you do when something like that happens to you? Well, honey, first you try to get the charge for the WiFi removed from your credit card. Bitch, you're on a budget now!

Next, you realize that some things just aren't meant to be, no matter how badly you want them.

Finally, you look around and realize that life is pretty fucking great already, so order another free champagne, look out the window, and "take a little time to enjoy the view."

CHAPTER FOUR

The Rosie O'Donnell Story

Rosé O'Donnell

1 bottle of Irish Rosé. I know, I know—wine isn't technically a "cocktail," but Dr. Dre isn't technically a doctor and I don't hear you complaining about that, do I?

Twice-Baked Cutie Potatatoes

2 russet potatoes

1 cup sour cream

½ cup ranch dressing

¼ cube salted butter (room temperature)

1 cup grated sharp cheddar cheese

2 cups chopped broccoli

Chives

Salt and pepper, to taste

2 tablespoons sriracha

Place potatoes in an oven at 350° for one hour to bake. Allow to cool, then slice in half long ways and, using a spoon, scoop the insides into a bowl. Be careful not to harm the skins, as they'll be used later. Mix one-half of the sour cream (save the other half for later), ranch dressing, butter, cheese, broccoli, chopped chives, and salt and pepper to taste. Fill the potato skins with the mixture, place on a baking sheet, and bake another 15 minutes at 350°.

While they're cooking, mix the remaining sour cream with the sriracha. Once your Twice-Baked Cutie Potatatoes are finished, top them with a dollop and enjoy!

ROSIE O'DONNELL ONCE made me sleep with a Republican.

Do I have your attention now? Yeah, I bet. I'll get to that a little later, but first let me explain why I love Rosie so much.

Have you ever known something to be true—in your soul—without having any facts at all to back it up? You just know without a doubt, as sure as you know that the sun will rise, tomorrow will come, and you'll scrap your New Year's resolution on or around January 3?

Well, growing up, I just *knew* that I would be friends with Rosie O'Donnell.

Sure, she'd been in mega-hit movies like *Sleepless in Seattle* and *A League of Their Own*, but it was her daily talk show that really hooked me. If you never watched *The Rosie O'Donnell Show*, boy, did you miss out. Immediately after it debuted in 1996, it was a huge hit—the kind of hit they don't really have on TV anymore. Every day, millions of us rushed home to spend an hour with our best friend, Rosie. She was hysterical, relatable, and always fanning out over big celebrities just like you or I would. She seemed like one of "us." Like if we bumped shopping carts at Target, we'd totally hit it off, you know?

Yes, Rosie had shot a Koosh ball right into this cutie patootie's li'l heart. I did whatever she said (watched *Ally McBeal* because she said it was good), bought whatever she said (I still feel bad about elbowing that lady in the face for the last Tickle Me Elmo in Toys R Us), and supported everything she did ("Sorry, fellas, I'd love to go toss the ball around, but Rosie's hosting the Tony Awards tonight and I simply can't miss it!").

It just makes sense that, as a kid, I would identify with Rosie. Hosting my own talk show was always my ultimate dream, plus we were both gay and we were both stocky brunettes. But it went far beyond merely having a few things in common. I genuinely felt, deep within the very fiber of my being, that we would one day be friends. Yes, I realize that the majority of her viewing audience probably felt this way—after all, that was a huge part of her magic, the reason her show was such a hit—but I was certain we would not only meet but really hit it off. I felt it in my gut—my soft, fifteen-year-old, Burger King–lovin' gut.

It turns out that, unlike the time I thought using an entire tub of self-tanner right before prom was a good idea, this time I was actually right.

To be honest, things didn't start out so great. Throughout high school, despite sending dozens of handwritten letters on my signature Lisa Frank stationery—reserved for only the most important correspondence—addressed to Studio 8G in NBC's Rockefeller Center Studio in New York City, inviting Rosie to come see me in my school musical or just to come over for snacks after school (even back then I made a mean crudité), I never heard back. I used to fantasize about her coming to surprise me on opening night. I remember starring as Henry Higgins in *My Fair Lady* during my junior year of high school (people are still buzzing about my timeless performance) and being distracted, looking in the corner to see if Ms. O'Donnell would sneak in, stand in the back of the darkened theater, and wipe away a single tear during my soul-wrenching rendition of "I've Grown Accustomed to Her Face."

So, that never happened, but nevertheless I persisted.

Cut to the year 2006. *Ugly Betty* had us all glued to the TV, Shakira's "Hips Don't Lie" had us all shaking our booties, and the classic film *Big Momma's House 2* had us all wondering, "Is this the year Martin Lawrence *finally* wins an Oscar?"

I was four years into my stint as Ross the Intern on *The Tonight Show with Jay Leno*. After my success covering the 2002 Winter Olympics in Salt Lake City (and by "success" I mean I avoided dropping an F-bomb or slipping on the ice), the producers decided to once again send me to cover the games, this time in

Torino, Italy. Italy?!? Oh wow! As a lower-middle-class farm boy, I never thought I'd ever get to go to Italy, the home of Michelangelo's *David*, the Leaning Tower of Pisa, and, most importantly, the birthplace of endless soup, salad, and breadsticks (shout-out to Olive Garden!).

At the time, an exciting new thing called blogging was just taking off, and one of the first celebrities to start blogging was Rosie O'Donnell. This was after her talk show ended in 2002, but before she started on *The View* later in 2006, so it was a way for me to still get my daily dose of my Rosie. I was obsessed with checking Rosie.com every single morning. She'd post pictures of her house in Miami, write poems about Joni Mitchell, and answer fan questions in her "Ask Ro" section. She was more unedited and raw than I'd ever seen a star of her caliber be before. She even swore. I fuckin' loved it!

Motivated by what Rosie was doing, I approached the head honchos at NBC.com about doing my own blog, one chronicling my experience covering the Olympics in Torino. They loved the idea, although they told me there was no budget for it. Who cares? Let's face it, I'll never win an award for my business savvy. Even as a kid, when I had my paper route, I did it more to socialize than to monetize.

Italy is beautiful. Italians do everything with style. Everything is sexy: The architecture, the food, the people, although they did make fun of me when I asked for ranch dressing to dip my pizza in. I may not speak Italian, but I can understand a judgmental eye-roll in any language. To quote Michelle Tanner from *Full House*, "How rude!" (or "*Che maleducato!*" in Italian).

So in between interviewing the latest Olympian gold medal winner and trying my hand at speed skiing (honey, it was all downhill from there!), I'd take pictures and write blog entries documenting my Italian trip of a lifetime. NBC was great about promoting it, and after mentioning it on air the first night of our *Tonight Show* coverage, it became a bona fide hit. Thousands and thousands of people began reading my blog every day and leaving their two cents in the comments section. I couldn't believe it! In one entry, I shared how I had been inspired by Rosie to start the blog. I can only assume that one of my "blog buddies" must've also been a regular reader of Rosie's blog and told her about it, because the next day when I did my usual routine of checking Rosie.com, I couldn't believe what I saw.

Rosie had written a blog entry, talking about the usual—her kids and crafting. But at the end of it, I saw something else. Something I couldn't believe. There in black-and-white, Rosie had ended her entry with "Oh, and I love Ross the Intern."

I must have read that sentence at least a hundred times, making sure she really meant me. *Maybe she was referring to the discount clothing store Ross Dress for Less or David Schwimmer's character on* Friends? No, it clearly said "the Intern" after "Ross." She was talking about me!

Right after that, I checked the comment section of my own blog and saw a comment on the entry I had written about Rosie from a user named—are you ready?—Rosie. She said, "Love u, kid."

Now I know that the internet—and specifically blog comment sections—are chock-full of people pretending to be someone else—but I just *knew* it was really her.

And you know what? I was totally right. It was her! A couple of months after the Olympics, Rosie was scheduled to be a guest on *The Tonight Show*, and the producer of her segment told me, "Hey, Rosie is gonna be a guest on the show next week and she told me she wants you to come hang in her dressing room before the show."

Say what? Rosie O'NoSheDidn't! The producer said it so casually that it almost didn't register, as if he was telling me something boring and basic like, "Your dry cleaning is ready for pickup" or "Doing your taxes is important."

This was huge. Talk about a *Charlie and the Chocolate Factory* moment! This was my golden ticket and I knew it! There was only one thing that worried me—the one thing that almost always worried me: What would I wear?

Of course I opted for the Rosie.com T-shirt I had ordered from her online store. It was comfortable, showed respect for my talk show she-ro, and was roomy enough to allow for some serious emotional eating should things go south.

The day of Rosie's appearance on *The Tonight Show*, I hesitated before knocking on her dressing room door. Now, I rarely get nervous. Usually when something momentous is about to happen, I take a deep breath, brace myself, and dive right in without any fear. This was not one of those times. Despite knowing we were destined to be friends and the fact that I was a twenty-six-year-old man, I found myself having a flashback to being that fifteen-year-old kid watching Rosie from my small farm town, dreaming of the moment we'd meet. This was finally that moment. Would it go okay? I'd be lying if I said I wasn't worried.

Turns out I had nothing to worry about.

I knocked on her door and heard that familiar, world-famous voice with the no-nonsense Long Island accent yell, "Ross!!! Get in here!"

She gave me a big hug and made me feel instantly at ease. We talked as if we had known each other forever. She asked me a ton of questions about myself. I almost felt like I was a guest on her show. The more inquisitive she got, the more interesting I became. I felt like I was a hit! It suddenly became very clear why she was so good at what she did.

Let me tell you something about famous people—they are always physically smaller in real life than they appear on TV or in the movies. Rosie was no exception. For such a force of nature, she was kind of teeny-tiny. What also struck me was how perfect her teeth were. I know, I'm meeting one of my all-time idols and I'm staring at her teeth? But they were so white! Who was her dentist? What really stood out to me most, though, was how innately maternal she was. She held my clammy hand, called me "kid," and was just so naturally nurturing, calming, and warm.

We had talked for quite a while, really bonding, when the unthinkable happened. Out of nowhere, Rosie gave me the gift celebrities don't give just anyone. No, not the solid gold key to the private celebrity bathroom (I'm still waiting for that!). For famous people, it is the one thing held most sacred—the thing they only give to those they feel they can trust, those who have been deemed worthy of being welcomed into the inner circle that is their precious private lives. On those rare occasions when a connection clearly crosses from fan and into friend, a celebrity will give you: their personal email and telephone number.

And, yeah, not to brag, but Rosie totally gave me her digits! *Holla!* And I gave her mine (which was much less significant since I gave my number to anyone I had known for more than five minutes).

Having your idol's telephone number and email address can be dangerous. I was determined to respect this honor, to think before I leapt. Unlike the very first time I encountered one of those three-story chocolate fondue fountains surrounded by fruit and chunks of pound cake at a buffet table, I didn't want to go hog wild and completely embarrass myself (you guys, they called security). So I waited for Rosie to make the first move. I didn't have to wait long.

July 25, 2006

> hey u
> its me
> Rosie

Wow. I sat down and wrote out a long email, thanking her for the day we spent together in her dressing room. I also couldn't let the moment pass without getting a little sentimental. Here's how I closed my email.

> At the risk of sounding a little mushy, I need to tell you that I'm just a kid from Mount Vernon, Washington, and the fact that I just got an email from you will never not be surreal and too much for me to take. Watching you and your show during my formative years is why I'm doing what I'm doing—I said to myself, "That's what I want to do. That's what I'm meant to do. She inspires me."
>
> Too mushy? Oh well, I can't help it—it's true.
>
> Love,
> Ross

I held my breath. Friendship, like dating, is a two-way street. All you can do is express how you feel and hope the other person at the very least respects your honesty. But there's always the chance of going too far, too soon, and scaring someone away. Had I said too much? Been too vulnerable?

Her response, in typical form, was perfect.

listen
every time i go out to dinner
or get a phone call from bette midler
my heart starts beating fast
my palms sweat
i get it

u r very good at being u ross
excited fun kind and full of life
keep doing it

xx
rosie

Gotta love her. Not only was she sweet and supportive, but she was a Bette Midler fan to boot? I mean, come on! Our friendship just grew from there. We continued emailing regularly for months. While the rest of the world was reading Rosie's daily blog, I was now getting the unfiltered Rosie on a regular basis. In the summer of 2007, Rosie went on tour with Cyndi Lauper and her True Colors tour and invited me to come hang with them when the show stopped in Las Vegas. Her treat! Faster than you could say "Girls Just Wanna Have Fun," I screamed "YES!"

The next thing I knew I was at the MGM Grand Hotel in the front row with Rosie as the iconic Cyndi Lauper sang mere feet in front of us. After the show, Rosie and I went backstage and she introduced me. "Ro, you wanna go out?" Cyndi asked. I made a mental note to nonchalantly call Rosie "Ro" one day soon.

"Sure," Rosie answered. I assumed this was my time to exit stage left. Rosie and Cyndi—two superstars—were gonna go out for a night on the town, and now it was time for Li'l Ross to go to bed.

Rosie turned to me. "Ross, let's all go!"

I hadn't felt this popular since a senior girl asked me to prom when I was just a sophomore. I just hope Rosie didn't have a crush on me like that sweet but clueless girl did! Of course I tagged along as we went downstairs to the True Colors after-party at Studio 54 in the MGM.

At this point in 2007, I was no stranger to red carpets. Having worked on *The Tonight Show* for more than six years, I had covered dozens of them. But this was different. When we arrived at the party, there was a red carpet outside with photographers' bulbs flashing as they took pictures of the stars arriving. "Rosie, Cyndi, Ross—this way," they yelled. *They know my name?* I kept trying to pull away and allow the press to get what they wanted—a two-shot of Rosie and Cyndi—but Rosie held me tight. She knew what she was doing, and I was so grateful—she was making me feel like I belonged.

The after-party was sponsored by the incredible LGBTQ organization the Human Rights Campaign, so we were surrounded by people who, like us, were fighting for very important issues like marriage equality, which, at this point, was still just a dream. Cyndi's song "True Colors" had been a number-one hit back in 1986, and now, twenty-one years later, it had taken on a whole new meaning. The Bush administration had literally just tried to amend the constitution to define "marriage" as a union between a man and a woman, ensuring that gay people would never, ever have the right to marry. Our community was under attack. Walking down that red carpet in solidarity was fun, but it also felt important.

If you Google it, you will see photos of us from that night. There is one in particular where I am actually sitting on Rosie's lap. It's one of the few times in my life when I was so skinny I could sit on someone's lap without it resulting in a hip replacement for them or an injury lawsuit against me (thanks, *Celebrity Fit Club*).

I felt great! I must've been oozing confidence, too, because a really cute guy started flirting with me. His name was Brian and he was very handsome—Asian with thick, dark hair, a deep voice, and the kind of jawline you only see on the covers of romance novels. People, how is it that I can somehow smell a freshly baked Krispy Kreme donut from a mile away, but I can't seem to recognize full-fledged flirting from five feet away? Obviously, I'm blessed with the Decorative Throw Pillow Gene and the Remembering Julia Roberts Quotes from *Steel Magnolias* Gene, but sadly not the all-important Flirting Gene.

Because of my complete and utter lack of this natural skill, I just assumed this hot guy was smiling at Rosie and Cyndi. But later, even after I introduced him to them, he remained focused on me. Rosie noticed, too, whispering, "That cutie patootie is totally flirting with you!"

Uh-oh. I'm so bad at this. The last time anyone had flirted with me was when I was on the phone with a male customer service rep for the cable company. We hit it off big time. Before we hung up, he gave me free HBO and said, "Ma'am, you sure sound like a lot of fun." (You bet your sweet cable box I am, sir!)

But Rosie was right. This hottie was totally into me! He must have had some sort of fetish for painfully perky previously porky people, and I was perfectly pleased with it! As the party was winding down, we all walked outside to get into our cars and head back to the hotel where Rosie and I were staying.

Our SUV and his cab pulled up at the same time. Just as I turned to say good night, he asked if I wanted to go out. I had come with Rosie and you know what they say—"Leave with the Lesbian You Came With." (That's a Jonathan Adler pillow just waiting to be mass-produced, am I right?)

Out of respect for Rosie, I said no. I thought it was the right thing to do.

Rosie thought I was crazy. "Are you crazy?" she yelled as she shoved me toward him and into his waiting cab. "You are going out with him!"

"But . . ." I tried to protest.

"Go!" When Rosie O'Donnell yells "Go" at you, you go. And I'm so glad I did. We had a blast, hitting up a couple gay bars, having a few drinks, and talking late into the night. Around midnight he asked if I wanted to go home with him.

Now, normally I would never do this. But I feel like you and I have really bonded by this point in the book, and we're all adults here (unless your "cool mom" bought you this book, in which case I'd like to be friends with your mom). Uncle Ross is gonna break it down for you: When two people love each other—or even just like each other or don't really know each other but one of them has a really strong jawline and the other had a really strong piña colada—they sometimes go into a room together, take off their clothes, and get to know each other better. Don't you dare judge me. I'm human. I have needs!

They say that what happens in Vegas stays in Vegas, except for the seven pounds you pack on from the buffet, and out-of-character hookups that end up here in print for the whole world to see. So, yes, you dragged it out of me—me and the Hot Asian spent the night together. I hope you're not expecting a couple pages of juicy, *Fifty Shades of Gay* details. It's not that kind of book. Like, I would never ever tell you that IT WAS REALLY, REALLY GOOD. Ever. I don't kiss and tell.

When I woke up the next morning, he was standing across the room in his underwear—the teeny-tiny kind of underwear people like me will never wear because, let's face it, there isn't enough dieting, exercise, or liposuction in the world. He was gorgeous, but he was also sweet. *Maybe, just maybe,* I thought, *this could be more than a one-night stand. Maybe I just hit the jackpot in Vegas.*

While I was watching his hot body and deciding on a color scheme for our upcoming celebrity-studded wedding on Fire Island, he was watching the morning news on TV. He looked so sexy that I couldn't help but start hoping for Round Two, but President Bush was speaking and—I'm sorry, but there's no nice way to say this—that is the ultimate boner-killer.

As "W" blabbed on and on, I rolled my eyes and let out a sigh of disgust. And that's when my hot date let me know that there would be no fabulous same-sex wedding in our future, let alone a second date. "I love Bush."

Oh, good! I thought. *Now I don't need to manscape anymore!*

"I'm serious," he said, very seriously. And then he dropped the bomb. "I'm a Republican."

Huh? Excuse me? Come again? I lay there in bed, so confused. I'm sorry, but when a guy says, "Let's take the party back to my room," you don't think he means the Republican Party.

Wow. Now, I get along with just about everyone. I'd been with women (okay, just the one in high school) and men of all shapes and sizes and races. But he was my first real live Republican. *OMG*, I thought. *Am I totally bi? Bipartisan! I'm like a Goodwill Ambassador! Awesome!!!*

That was over ten years ago, and now our country is even more divided. Right, Left, Red, Blue . . . God, it sounds like the most boring game of Twister ever, right? But maybe, just maybe, if more people would simply reach across the aisle to embrace (or even more than just embrace, if you know what I mean!) their political foe, there would be a whole lot more love in this world.

Am I a national hero? Maybe. But that's not for me to say. That's not a title you can give yourself. But if you said it, I wouldn't argue with you. I just know that I look back on that night in Vegas with no regrets. I took a gamble. I rolled the dice with a roll in the hay. I went all in, and, in my opinion, I was a winner. I'd like to think I did my part that night to Make America Great (In Bed) Again. You're welcome, America.

The next morning, Ro called me for all the juicy details. And just like girlfriends do, I told her everything. Well, almost everything. I never told her that she made me sleep with a Republican. I honestly didn't know if she could take it.

CHAPTER FIVE

The Seahawks Love Story

COCKTAIL

The 12th Man

1 ounce vodka

Equal parts Fresca and blue Powerade Zero

Add ice and drink it during every Seattle Seahawks game like I do. Then spike your cup in the end zone while doing your favorite touchdown dance.

Football Meatballs

1 bag frozen meatballs (beef, turkey, whatever)

1 container barbeque sauce

1 container sour cream

1 bag shredded lettuce

Put meatballs in an oven at 350° with barbeque sauce until heated through—roughly twenty minutes. Toss and make sure all the meatballs are covered. Cover a serving dish with shredded lettuce and place the meatballs on it. Then fill a plastic sandwich bag with sour cream, squeezing the sour cream into a corner. Using scissors, cut the very tip of the corner of the bag. Using both hands, squeeze the bag and draw football lines on each meatball. Now they look like footballs on a football field! Genius, I know!

IT SHOCKS MOST people when they find out that I'm a die-hard football fan, but I am. Like, legit. I even shell out a few hundred buckaroos every year for the NFL Red Zone Channel so I can watch every game live as they're happening. I'm hard-core, man. But it wasn't always that way. As a kid, the only "super bowl" I cared about was the oversized serving dish I ate my Froot Loops out of. (Side note: It's just dawning on me, literally at this very moment, that they probably spelled "fruit" as "froot" because it didn't actually contain *any* real fruit! And I thought I was being so healthy!)

My obsession with football started when I was a kid and

had absolutely nothing else to talk about with my straight older brother and even straighter dad. Every Sunday during football season I had two choices: I could either sit in awkward silence as they watched the big game or join in on the fun. I chose to join in! As my dad guzzled cheap Schmidt beer, I sipped my Diet Shasta Root Beer. And every time the kicker missed a game-winning field goal, making my brother give the living room wall a punch, I would do a shot of the "hard stuff"—Hawaiian Punch.

If you're from the Seattle area, you're undoubtedly all about Starbucks, Seasonal Affective Disorder, and the Seattle Seahawks. I always say there are no fair-weather Seahawks fans, and not just because there is no fair weather in Seattle. No, being a Seahawks fan wasn't always easy. The Hawks joined the NFL as an expansion team (fancy football talk for "brand-new") in 1976, the same year our great nation celebrated two hundred years of freedom and liberty. And it took the team almost that long to finally make it to the Super Bowl. They eventually got to the big game in 2005, only to lose 21–10 to the Pittsburgh Steelers. I'm still not over it. The Pittsburgh Steelers? More like the Dream Stealers!

Cut to 2013. It was a good time to be alive—Obama had just been reelected, Anne Hathaway had just won an Oscar, and my career was going great! I was appearing weekly on E!'s hit talk show *Chelsea Lately*, starring my friend Chelsea Handler. I loved being on the rotating commentary panel each week alongside hilarious people like Whitney Cummings, Loni Love, Heather McDonald, Josh Wolf, and Sarah Colonna, among others.

And just when I thought 2013 couldn't get any better, it totally did. Just imagine the excitement Seahawks fans felt that year when it seemed like the team had the magical lineup and momentum to finally bring the elusive Lombardi Trophy home to Seattle. It just felt right, like when Heather Locklear joined *Melrose Place*. You could feel it in the air, like a shimmering golden ray of sunshine bursting through the gray Pacific Northwestern sky: This was our year.

I don't want to brag, but I will. Over the years, I've tweeted so much about the Seahawks that the team has actually taken notice and we've become friendly on social media. Check it out. @Seahawks totally follows @HelloRoss. Their public relations people took notice, too, and invited me that season to the NFC Championship game against the San Francisco 49ers. This was the deciding game as to who would be going to the Super Bowl. If we lost, we were done. If we won, we were in!

I was so excited. Remember, I was used to watching the games at home with the aforementioned beer-guzzling and wall-punching. The one time I did attend a live game as a kid, we sat on a cold, hard bench in the nosebleed section. I could barely enjoy my overpriced crappy snacks because it was so freezing, my teeth were chattering like one of those windup novelty toys that look like a set of possessed dentures.

Now I was quite literally in the lap of a luxury box. Not only did I get to sit in a very fancy booth (toasty overhead heaters, free-flowing cocktails, and bottomless nachos, oh my!) but before and during the game I got to stand on the sidelines and watch the action—not to mention quarterback Russell Wilson in his skintight pants—up close and personal. Um, wow. Just wow.

It was during halftime when Seahawks player #9, punter Jon

Ryan, approached me on the sidelines. Now, Jon wasn't just any punter. He hailed from Canada and was very good-looking—a real Saskatchewan Don Juan. A poutine-lovin' punter! He's from a town named Regina, which always makes me giggle because in Canada, when pronounced correctly, it rhymes with a certain lady part. Gets me every time! #SooryNotSoory

With nearly ten years in the NFL under his belt, Jon was also a Seahawks team captain, having finished the regular season with seventy-four punts for 3,159 net yards and a 42.69 average, although he was anything but average. And now he was approaching me with a big smile on his face.

"Hey, Ross!" he said, spinning a football in his giant, Canadian hands. "Big fan here. I watch *Chelsea Lately* every night. I'm Jon Ryan, the punter."

Umm, duh. I knew exactly who he was.

"Umm, duh. I know exactly who you are!"

He laughed. "The show is so funny. And you've gotta hook me up with Sarah Colonna. I've got a huge crush on her."

I could see why. Sarah was hilarious and gorgeous and, to my knowledge, completely single.

And here's where I should confess something to you. The idea of matchmaking has always appealed to me. I've always dreamed of introducing two people who eventually get married. Why? For many reasons. Of course I want people to be happy. Of course I want to see a beautiful union between two lovely people flourish. But mostly I've always wanted to go to a wedding that I didn't have to pay for, but was still all about me.

"Oh, Ross, how wonderful! Look what *you* did! *You're* amazing! Here, have another scrumptious goat-cheese-and-fig canapé! And how about a free glass of champagne? No, here, have the good stuff—not that cheap crap we're serving the regular guests! And for dinner *you* can have the chicken *and* the fish—*you* don't have to choose! We've seated you right next to the life-sized ice sculpture of you. Oh, and do you want a piece of wedding cake? I know the bride and groom haven't cut it yet, but I don't think they'd mind. After all, they wouldn't even be here if it weren't for *you*! We're all here because of *YOU*!"

God, that sounds great.

So when Seahawks punter #9 Jon Ryan asked me to introduce him to my friend Sarah Colonna, I couldn't help but think, *OMG, this is my "in" to matchmaking! Here's your shot, Ross! Introduce them, they can get married, live happily ever after, throw a wedding in your honor, and name their first child Ross, regardless of its gender!* It was perfect!

But if he wanted me to hook him up with my friend Sarah, I wanted something, too. He wanted to win her heart? Fine. But first, he'd just have to fulfill one simple request.

"Okay." I put my hands on the sides of his Seahawks helmet and stared him squarely in the eye through the facemask. "Tweet me and I will tell Sarah that she should date you . . . but only if you win this game."

"Deal." We shook hands. It may not have been a legally binding contract, but we both meant business and I'm confident any court in the land would've upheld our deal.

"Now go win this game!" He ran off with an extra spring in his step. I was tempted to try to smack his butt like all the players did to motivate each other, but I didn't think we were there quite yet.

Yes, I had just pimped out my friend to win a football game, and I was fine with it. I went back to the luxury box to continue watching the second half, sitting on pins and needles despite the overstuffed recliner that cradled my nervous body. I was sweating like Paris Hilton on *Celebrity Jeopardy!* I was so nervous I could barely touch my gourmet cheese-and-herb popcorn and complimentary Chardonnay. It was awful.

It was touch and go until the very end of the game. A real nail-biter, and I had just gotten a manicure! And then, with just twenty-five seconds remaining, the Seahawks leading 23–17, Seattle's Richard Sherman tipped a Colin Kaepernick pass in the end zone and teammate Michael Smith intercepted, ensuring the Seahawks' win and earning them a spot in Super Bowl XLVIII.

The crowd went insane. I lost my freaking mind. I was sitting next to Seattle native and famous white rapper (or "whapper," as I call them) Macklemore and we actually hugged. We never spoke before or after that, but hugged in that moment, and since then I've always had a sinking suspicion that his hit song "Glorious" is about me. It turns out football is the universal language.

The next day I checked Twitter and there was a tweet from #9, Jon Ryan. He was calling my bluff, and I had every intention of following through on my promise. Jon had punted, and now the ball was in my court, which I understand is mixing two different sports. I retweeted his tweet, adding, "Hey @SarahColonna, you should date this guy. He's gonna win the Super Bowl."

A couple weeks later, the Seahawks went on to crush the Denver Broncos 43–8, winning the Super Bowl for the first time and bringing pride to fans everywhere. Well, everywhere other than Denver. It was huge. I painted my face blue and green, and for once it was not part of an extensive skincare regime. WOO HOO! The end.

What? Why are you still reading? The Hawks won the big

game! What else is there to say? Oh, Sarah and Jon's lifetime of happiness? Oh, okay. If you really wanna know, I can tell you what happened, but if the big Super Bowl win is enough for you, then stop reading right now and just skip to the next chapter.

Okay, so for those of you who have decided to stay, there are two possible endings to the Sarah & Jon story . . .

- **ENDING #1:** I told Sarah that she should date this Canadian football player that she had never met and she just laughed it off and they never met. End of story.

- **ENDING #2:** They actually started tweeting each other and totally hit it off! Then they actually met up in person! And then they actually started dating! And then every time I saw Sarah she would thank me profusely. "He's amazing! I think I'm in love!"

So which is it? Ending #1 or Ending #2? Yep, you're right. Sadly, it's Ending #1, so I guess the lesson here is—JUST KIDDING, YOU JADED, CYNICAL, NEGATIVE PERSON WHO CLEARLY DOESN'T BELIEVE IN LOVE, MAGIC, FAIRY TALES, AND HAPPILY-EVER-AFTERS!

It was Ending #2! They totally fell in love! And all thanks to me!

It was a great reminder of a life lesson that I think we all too often forget: I AM AMAZING! Look what I did! I introduced two people and now they're dating! I was one step closer to becoming Millionaire Matchmaker Patti Stanger!

And just when I thought it couldn't get any better, months later Sarah and Jon asked me to meet up with them at a Mexican restaurant for happy hour. Umm, of course! Happy hour is my favorite hour of them all! When I showed up, they were already cozied up in a booth, looking cuter than could be. I was so happy for them . . . and, of course, happy for myself. We hugged and caught up for a few minutes then moved on to the most important part of a Mexican restaurant experience: the chips and salsa. Jon reached for a chip, and a shimmer caught my eye. I let out a scream . . . I hadn't seen it until then, but knew what it was immediately: Jon had worn his Super Bowl ring. Right there in front of me was the holy grail of NFL achievements, and the mother of all statement jewelry.

Instantly, I leaned in about a quarter-inch from his ring finger and began inspecting it with pride. "Look at that! There's a little Seahawks logo made out of diamonds! Amazing!"

Jon was beaming. "You wanna wear—?"

Before he could finish the question, I ripped it off his finger, put it on mine, and began snapping selfies of myself to send to my brother. This was gonna kill him. No, seriously . . . If I knew my brother, he'd be so jealous, a wall was bound to get punched.

Wearing the ultimate NFL outfit accessory was a dream come true, but it wasn't my ultimate fantasy. No, what I really wanted was to meet my full matchmaker potential. I needed Jon and Sarah to get married. So imagine my joy when another ring was revealed to me that night, this time on Sarah's hand. They were engaged! TOUCHDOWN!

Even though Sarah wouldn't let me try on her ring (whatever), I was ecstatic. Two wonderful friends of mine had fallen in love and made the decision to commit to each other for life. It was beautiful. AND IT WAS ALL BECAUSE OF ME!!! I was finally going to have the wedding of my dreams! Assuming, of course, I was invited.

"Ross, we want to ask you something." Sarah shifted, getting serious. "We're getting married in Mexico in July and we've discussed it. Please don't feel obligated, but we'd love it if you could officiate the wedding."

OMG. This was too good to be true. A wedding in my honor and I got the lead role?!? I was all in.

All kidding aside, the wedding was gorgeous, and not about me at all, of course. Jon beamed as Sarah, stunning in a sleeveless Michal Medina gown, walked onto the beach in Los Cabos, Mexico, in front of all their friends and family. Their vows made me cry. And in all sincerity, having the honor of officiating their nuptials is something I'll carry with me for the rest of my life.

Oh, and the appetizers were *muy delicioso*!

Love, like football, is a contact sport that requires a lot of heart. You make a pass and just hope that someone catches it. And even though there may be some fouls along the way, you've got to have your teammate's back. You also should hydrate, stretch, and wear a cup at all times. Jon and Sarah are now co-captains of their own team, and my money's on them to win the big game of life.

CHAPTER SIX

The Brandi Glanville Story

COCKTAIL

Three bottles of white wine (keep reading and you'll see why . . .)

ROSSIPE

An Everything bagel with cream cheese (again, keep reading . . .)

I LOVE A good magazine quiz. You know, harmless self-centered fluff to keep you entertained while you're getting a pedicure. Important scientific inquiries like *"What Does Your Favorite Rihanna Song Reveal About Your Personality?"* or *"What Does Your Boyfriend's Favorite Friends Character Say About the Real Him?"*

Well, did you know that your favorite Real Housewife also says a lot about you, too? It's true! So go ahead and pick your favorite, but choose wisely . . .

> **NeNe Leakes:** You crave long, drawn-out drama and short, asymmetrical hairstyles.

> **Teresa Giudice:** You like throwing shade almost as much as you like throwing tables.

> **Lisa Vanderpump:** You love gargantuan diamonds and teeny-tiny dogs.

> **Brandi Glanville:** Oh, girl, you messy!

My personal result? Hi, I'm messy, too. Nice to meet you. I'm full-on Team Brandi Glanville and I don't even care. Years before she and I were holed up together in the *Celebrity Big Brother* house, I had a very, very bonkers Brandi Glanville experience that I've told only a select few friends . . . until now.

And just so you know, this entire chapter has Brandi's seal of approval. Are you kidding me? I'm not crazy enough to cross her! So I did the responsible thing and called her to get her blessing. No joke: I called her right before I began writing this chapter. We literally hung up just before I wrote this. It was the right thing to do.

Here's a transcript of our actual conversation:

RING . . . RING . . . RING . . .

Brandi Glanville: Oh, my God, is Ross Mathews actually calling me?

Me: Hilarious. How are you, baby?

BG: I'm good. Just headed home from the doctor 'cuz I fucked my neck up. Now my neck is filled with stem cells. I asked them to put them in my face, too, but they said they don't do that.

Me: No! Enough with the face. You look great. Stop.

BG: We'll see. What's up?

Me: So, I'm writing a book and I want to include a chapter about you.

BG: Oh, Jesus.

Me: Don't worry. The book isn't mean. But . . . okay, so I wanna write about that time you came over to the house.

BG: Fuck. (*Laughter.*)

Me: Look. It's all about how crazy you are, which is exactly why I love you so much.

BG: I don't care. Write whatever you want. I trust you. Plus, I don't even really remember what happened, so I'll get to find out when I read it.

Me: You're a mess! Love you!

BG: Love you, too. Bye.

Okay, so now that we have her seal of approval, let's do this. Brandi actually is my favorite Real Housewife—because she's hilarious, always serves up the drama that we viewers need, and she's the only one whose boobs I've seen in person! (Wait . . . I'm thinking . . . yes. She's the only one.)

I'll start at the beginning, which, according to Julie Andrews in *The Sound of Music*, is "a very good place to start!"

Back in 2013, Brandi and I had the same literary agent, Michael Broussard. I was busy writing my first (best-selling!) book, *Man Up!*, and Michael kept telling me, "Brandi Glanville just loves you. I've got to get you two together."

I was totally in. I had always thought Brandi was so funny and felt like if we ever met we would really hit it off. She just seemed like my kind of person: Fun and outrageous, but I could tell there was also a lot of heart underneath those knockout knockers. So one day Michael called me and said, "Brandi's on the line, too!"

This was my first three-way with one of the Real Housewives, but it didn't have to be my last! (Are you listening, Kyle and Mauricio?)

Just as I suspected, Brandi and I clicked right away. "You just make me happy!" she told me.

Well, that made *me* happy. We scheduled happy hour immediately, and unlike most Hollywood types, she actually followed through. We met up at a bar in the Valley, and I brought my partner at the time, Salvador, with me. Well, right away Brandi liked him better. "You're fine, Ross, but I love Salvador."

Fucking Brandi. She's always honest. And, truth be told, I loved seeing them get along so well. At the time, Salvador's career as a celebrity wardrobe stylist was really beginning to blossom, and the moment Brandi heard this, her natural inclination to support someone she cared about kicked in.

"Oh, my God," Brandi exclaimed, "you have to style me for this season's opening credits of *Housewives!*"

Salvador was gobsmacked. This was a big deal and quite an opportunity for him. These opening montages at the beginning of every episode of *The Real Housewives* were iconic. Styling one of the most talked-about cast members would be huge!

As anyone who watches Brandi on TV knows, she is fiercely loyal and she loves hard. Well, she's the same way in real life—even with new friends she's just met. I already liked her, but when she did that for Salvador, I fell in love with her.

We set up a time for Brandi to come to our house one Sunday to try on a bunch of gorgeous outfits Salvador had chosen for her. Designer Jeff Lewis had recently converted our garage into Sal's new studio on an episode of Bravo's *Interior Therapy.* Did you see that episode? That was a weird experience. I thought I had signed up to be on a new home remodel show, and the next thing I knew Jeff Lewis was in my house telling me that I was the problem in my relationship. Umm, okay, Dr. Lewis . . . Did you get your PhD in psychology from the prestigious Credenza Community College? I guess I was expecting more *Interior* and a little less *Therapy*? More kitchen and less bitchin'? More backsplash and less backtalk? You get the point.

And at the end of the day, my useless garage was now a showpiece! This space that had once held a Honda Scooter was now all about Haute Couture.

Salvador prepared for his styling session with Brandi by meticulously steaming and organizing all the different looks he had carefully chosen just for her. Since this was happening at 11 a.m. on a Sunday, I did what I do best—I prepped by setting up an extensive breakfast brunch buffet. We all have our talents!

I woke up early and went to the grocery store for bagels, cream cheese, and a big fruit platter. (Big Fruit Platter, by the way, is my rapper name. "Big Fruit Platter in da hizzy!" Book me now for your sweet sixteen, *quinceañera*, or bat mitzvah.)

As I headed to the cashier to check out, I passed the wine section and thought, *I know it's early on a Sunday morning, but maybe Brandi would like a glass of wine after trying on all those outfits. I mean, let's be honest, fashion can be exhausting.* So I picked up three bottles of pinot grigio—one for after the fitting if Brandi felt so inclined and two to just have in the house in case of emergency. What kind of emergency calls for a crisp white wine, you ask? An earthquake, a flood, or the sudden and unexpected announcement that Sarah Jessica Parker and Kim Cattrall have finally stopped feuding and agreed to do a third *Sex and the City* movie. Girl, I'm gonna need a drink when that happens.

Brandi arrived on time at 11 a.m. looking just as gorgeous as she does on TV, positively glowing in a simple white tank top and designer jeans. We all hugged and air-kissed and I offered her an Everything bagel covered in cream cheese because it was the polite thing to do (and because I didn't want to be the only one eating). Based on her reaction, though, you would've thought I had offered her a plate of fresh steaming dog poop. She curled her lip, violently shook her head, and said, "Oh, no no no, honey . . ."

I panicked. What had I done wrong? Did she have a gluten allergy? Was she lactose intolerant? Did her first boyfriend die in a freak accident in a bagel factory?

Brandi explained, "We don't do bread, sweetie."

Shit. I should've known that. Have you ever seen a Real Housewife eat a complex carbohydrate? Ever?!? Think, Mathews, think! Despite my faux pas with the Everything bagel, I hadn't done everything wrong. There was one thing on my breakfast buffet that was on Brandi's diet. You guessed it: She grabbed the bottle of wine and said, "But I will have some of this!"

We all laughed and I poured each of us a glass. We all clinked glasses—the only "toast" Brandi had that day.

Salvador got to work, holding up option after option. Brandi squealed with delight and began trying on clothes and drinking more wine, loosening up more and more with each outfit and each glass. It was like Brandi was our own real-life drunk Barbie doll! This was every little gay boy's dream come true, and it was happening in *our* house!

After a few drinks, Brandi stopped going into the little private changing room and, instead, began disrobing right in front of us. Whether we liked it or not, Salvador and I became very well acquainted with what we later dubbed *The Twins*. I learned two things that day: Brandi had great tits and—plot twist!—I'm a bit of a boob man.

As more outfits were rotated in and out, I noticed that her bra wasn't the only thing missing—the wine was gone, too. She held up the empty bottle and asked, "Do you have any more?"

Okay. I'm smart enough to know that when Brandi Glanville asks for more wine, you get her more wine. You guys, this was a wine emergency, and I was prepared! So I opened another bottle from my newly purchased stockpile, and she poured herself another glass. New dress, new glass of wine . . . new dress, new glass of wine . . . Her cups runneth over—and I'm not talking about her bra because, as I said, she was no longer wearing one.

I remember thinking, *Wow, Brandi can really hold her wine. She seems fine!* Frankly, I was really impressed—a heart of gold and a liver of steel! It was especially surprising since she's a very petite woman. Despite my voice, I am neither petite nor a woman, but if I drank that much wine I'd be a mess.

The second bottle of wine was now empty, and after three solid hours of plunging necklines, flowing hemlines, and bold prints, Brandi and Salvador finally decided on the perfect outfit to be immortalized in the opening credits of the upcoming season of *The Real Housewives of Beverly Hills*. Yay!

Brandi decided that the best way to celebrate this achievement was to leave the studio, march right into our kitchen in the main house . . . and open the third bottle of wine. At this point I felt a twinge of panic and didn't quite know what to do, but even though a word or two was being slurred here and there, Brandi still seemed okay, gabbing away and twirling in her new ensemble. It wasn't until about halfway through bottle number three that all that delicious fermented grape juice from some beautiful boutique winery in Sonoma suddenly hit poor Brandi like a ton of bricks. A ton of bricks with a fruity top note and an oaky finish.

Brandi attempted to lock eyes with me. "Where's my purse?" she asked, pronouncing the word *purse* as if it ended in several Zs.

Once we located her *purzzz*, she then proceeded to take out a bottle of pills and pop one in her mouth, washing it down with— you guessed it—more happy sauce.

Then she began transitioning in front of our eyes. Just like when Dr. Bruce Banner becomes the Incredible Hulk or when Miley Cyrus made her stunning transformation into larger-than-life Hannah Montana, Brandi shifted from sweet, normal girl into full-on friggin' Real Housewife mess. To put it bluntly, shit had just gotten real.

"What was that?" I asked, trying not to sound too concerned. But I was *very* concerned. After all, this tiny woman had just guzzled enough wine to quench the thirst of all the women on her Beverly Hills cast combined, with not even one bite of bagel in her stomach to help offset it. Girl, that's why brunch always features some sort of baked, sponge-like treat to soak up the booze: a scone, a biscuit, a muffin, A FUCKING BAGEL!

"It's just a Xanax," she said, rolling her eyes at me as if to say, "Jeez, Mom, relax!"

Just a Xanax!? Yeah, and I guess that J.Lo and Ben Affleck movie, Gigli, *was "just a bad idea"?*

After about twenty more minutes of outfit twirling, *purzzzzz* organization, and mumbled sentences, Brandi declared, "I'm tired."

As she felt her way down the hallway toward our bedroom, I hovered around her like an anxious mother with a child who is learning how to walk. Throughout the long, perilous journey down the ten-foot corridor, Brandi proceeded to take off all her clothes, leaving a breadcrumb-like trail of Dolce&Gabbana jeans and Zara tank top behind her. She finally crawled into the middle of our king-sized bed, burrowed under the covers like a glamorous little hibernating bear, and mumbled, "I'm gonna take a nap."

And, boy, did she nap. Every hour we would check in on her. 3 p.m., 4 p.m., 5 p.m. Still passed out. At about 6:30 p.m. I was legitimately worried, so I "accidentally" dropped a few pots and pans in the kitchen as Salvador ran into our bedroom to see if she woke up.

I asked Salvador, "Did she do anything?"

"Umm . . . sorta. She just sort of grunted and moved her head."

We have movement! That was a relief. "At least she's still alive."

At around 10 p.m., with Brandi still reigning as Queen of

Dreamland, I looked at Salvador. "Okay, I guess we should take the dogs and sleep out on the pull-out couch in the studio?"

You know, that Jeff Lewis sure comes in handy sometimes.

As we were falling asleep, Salvador whispered to me, "What do we do in the morning?"

"Well," I said, having already thought it out, "if she wakes up and apologizes, she's totally normal. If she wakes up and acts like this is nothing out of the ordinary, she's crazy as fuck."

We agreed and, squeezed onto a queen-sized sofa mattress with three dogs between us, somehow managed to fall asleep. If all that didn't make us "brunch hosts of the millennium," I didn't know what would.

At 6 a.m. the next morning, we heard a "knock, knock, knock" on our door. Brandi opened it and cheerfully exclaimed, "Good morning! I've gotta run. Thanks so much for yesterday—it was fun! Let's do it again. Have you seen my purse?"

Well, at least she can pronounce it properly this morning, I thought.

Exhausted, I pointed to her *purzzzzz* drunkenly strewn on the studio floor.

"Oh, there it is! Thanks again! See you both soon!"

"... Bye ...," Salvador and I said simultaneously, completely stunned. Brandi shut the door and gleefully went on her way.

"Okay, it's official," I said, looking at Salvador. "She's fucking nuts. And I love her!"

Salvador nodded. "Me, too."

And we're still friends to this day.

CHAPTER SEVEN

The Spice Girls Story

COCKTAIL

Zig-a-Zig Amaretto Sour

1½ ounces Amaretto liqueur

¾ ounce bourbon

1 ounce fresh lemon juice

1 teaspoon simple syrup (equal parts water and sugar, heated
until dissolved)

Combine Amaretto, bourbon, lemon juice, and simple syrup in a
shaker with ice and shake feverishly for about 30 seconds. Pour
into a glass and enjoy with at least four other friends.

Spiced Nuts

1 egg white

Whatever nuts you want—go nuts!

¾ cup sugar

1 tablespoon kosher salt

1 tablespoon chili powder

2 teaspoons cinnamon

2 teaspoons cayenne pepper

Whisk egg white, mix in nuts and dry ingredients, spread on a baking sheet prepared with nonstick spray, cook at 300° for 45 minutes, stirring occasionally.

EVERYONE REMEMBERS their first concert. Mine was the Spice Girls. I've always had great taste.

If I'm going to be totally honest, I've never been much of a concert person—too loud, too much standing, and don't even get me started on how long the lines are to buy some room-temperature, soggy $43 nachos. Sorry—it's just not my cup of processed cheese! But picture it: In 1998, I hear that the Spice Girls—my absolute favorite all-girl British pop global phenomenon—have a stop on their upcoming tour in a city just a few hours away. Honey, you'd better believe I "Wannabe" there!

I don't remember where I was the first time I heard that debut single in 1996. That's like trying to remember the first time I saw a sunrise, tasted a Starburst, discovered deep conditioner, or saw "Marky Mark" Wahlberg's Calvin Klein underwear ad. Who knows? I just remember it changed my life. I was instantly obsessed. The Spice Girls were so energetic, so outrageous, and so original. It was love at first sight.

For those of you with no taste who have no clue who the Spice Girls are, allow me to explain . . .

First of all, how dare you? Secondly, the Spice Girls were unprecedented—the best-selling girl group of all time, eventually selling upward of seventy-five million albums. Much like the Beatles before them, they were a British invasion who took over the world. Except they were the first all-female group to do it, and they brought with them a message of girl power and female empowerment, delivered in skintight vinyl pants and body glitter. Everywhere you looked—from awards shows to commercials to the radio to the movie theater—the Spice Girls had taken over. Um, did I just say the movie theater? Yes, that's right—they starred in their very own big-screen, big-budget movie, *Spice World*. Which was a very appropriate title because they had pretty much taken over the world . . . and, sugar, I was here for all that spice!

Truth be told, it wasn't easy growing up in a farm town as a chubby, somewhat awkward teenage boy with the voice of a middle-aged lady. Maybe that's why I felt such a connection to this group of outrageous, in-your-face adult women. I was attracted to much more than just their undeniably catchy pop songs. I was immediately drawn to their jubilant "Just be yourself" message that was evident in everything they did. They were each celebrated for what made them unique. As a unique kid myself, I found their confidence inspiring.

The main ingredients in the Spice Girls' recipe for success consisted of its five fierce and fabulous females:

- **Scary Spice:** Black, bold, and beautiful, Scary Spice (Mel B) was anything but scary. With her beautifully curly hair, pierced tongue, and catlike moves, she was scalding hot—but I guess Scalding Spice doesn't really roll off the tongue, so they went with Scary.

- **Sporty Spice:** Although her name sounds suspiciously like an antiperspirant, Sporty Spice (Mel C) was all about jazzy jogging suits and snazzy sneakers—which, incidentally, has become my signature look every weekend when I'm in Palm Springs. Sporty always looked like she had just ditched PE to do a concert.

- **Posh Spice:** True to her name, Posh Spice (Victoria Beckham—yes, the bitch stole my man, David) was the most subtle of the girls—upscale, expensive-looking, and classy. She also had the most perfectly blunt bob haircut I've ever seen. I love me a good bob!

- **Baby Spice:** Sweet and innocent, Baby Spice (Emma) was undeniably the sweetest of all the spices. Her youthful look of blond pigtails, rosy cheeks, and short pink skirts appealed to the Girls' younger fans—and I can only assume a handful of creepy old men who drove white vans.

- **Ginger Spice:** With her sequined Union Jack minidress, fiery red hair with a blond streak, and sky-high platform boots, Ginger Spice (Geri) had the most iconic look of all the Girls. Like her namesake spice, Ginger had a real kick!

I've always adored an all-female power posse, but whenever I try to identify with a favorite, I've always struggled to choose just one. For example, when it comes to *The Golden Girls*, I'm a Dorothy/Rose hybrid. But when it comes to the Spice Girls, the choice is clear—I'm a firm Ginger. One hundred percent. No question. She remains my favorite. Don't get me wrong, my sophisticated teen palate appreciated all the Spices, but the spice du jour that fed my hunger best was always Ginger.

Cut to my senior year of high school. Everyone who was anyone at Mount Vernon High School knew that I was a Spice Girl superfan. I was basically almost an honorary member. The sixth spice—Pumpkin Spice. Right after third period, as I was skipping to the cafeteria for lunch, my friend Molly ran up to me in the hallway. "Ross!" she yelled. "You're never gonna believe this!"

What? I thought. *Whatever it is must be big. The captain of the football team came out? We're doing* Bye Bye Birdie *for the spring musical? Hollywood got my letters and is* finally *making* Pretty Woman 2: Back on the Streets?

Molly continued, trying to catch her breath, "They're coming here . . . Just announced . . . Oh . . . my . . . God . . ."

I was in no mood for games. I didn't have time to dillydally. After all, it was Tater Tot Day in the cafeteria, and if Molly didn't spit it out soon, the line would be too long and I'd miss out. This couldn't happen. Not again! Not on my watch! I grew impatient. "What are you talking about?"

"The Spice Girls!" Molly screamed in my face. "They're coming to Washington in August!"

It's true what they say—when you're held up at gunpoint, when you're in a car accident, or when someone tells you that your favorite girl group is coming to a city near you—everything starts to move in slow motion. I could feel the linoleum floor falling out from beneath my feet and my face turning redder than Ginger Spice's hair. The Spice Girls are coming to town?!? Tater tots, schmater schmots! People, this was a historical moment! I mean, this was the very first—and last—time in my life that I was more interested in women than deep-fried potatoes.

I couldn't believe it. Faster than I could recite all the lyrics to "Say You'll Be There," the Spice Girls would be here.

I saved and saved to buy my tickets, sacrificing all modern luxuries. I practically became Amish. First, I immediately ceased all super-sizing of my value meals at McDonald's. Next, I stopped going to Blockbuster to rent movies and instead started suffering through movies on TV. You guys—do you know how many commercials I had to watch? And finally, I had to make the ultimate sacrifice and give up my favorite Bonne Bell Kiwi Strawberry Lip Smacker and settle for plain, flavorless, boring ol' budget-friendly ChapStick. It took years for my lips to recover.

But it was all worth it. Before I knew it, I had somehow managed to scrape together enough money to buy my ticket. I had to get to work: The concert was coming up at the Tacoma Dome on August 8, 1998, and those glittery, puffy-paint "I ♥ GINGER!" signs weren't gonna make themselves! And what to wear? I mean, I wanted an outfit that was fashionably festive, yet figure-friendly and flattering. But I also insisted on being respectful of the girls, so as not to steal focus away from them. And, most importantly, I wanted an outfit that would complement Ginger's signature red-and-blue Union Jack dress when she would see me in the audience, pluck me from the crowd, and pull me on stage to perform "Spice Up Your Life" with the Girls. Hello! I already knew the harmonies and choreography—it just made sense!

Little did I know, however, that despite all my planning and preparation, this Spice Girls concert would be a recipe for disaster.

There are certain events you remember where you were when they happened. Sunday, May 31, 1998, was one of those days. Bill Clinton was president. *Major League: Back to the Minors* was the number one VHS rental. The Chicago Bulls beat the Indiana Pacers 88–83. It seemed like a normal day. But it was anything but.

It was late Sunday evening, and I was mindlessly snacking on Funyuns while frantically doing the geometry homework I had avoided all weekend as the evening news played in the background. "Blah blah blah Monica Lewinsky . . . Blah blah blah impeachment . . . Blah blah blah Ginger Spice . . ."

WHAT?!? I turned up the TV.

The news anchor seemed to stare right at me, matter-of-factly through the screen. "Many are calling it 'the end of an era' . . . The popular pop group the Spice Girls have just announced today that member Geri Haliwell—better known as 'Ginger Spice'—will be leaving the group, effective immediately . . ."

Leaving the group? Does not compute. Maybe I had misheard the news anchor? My brain, in survival mode, kicked into full-blown denial and began making up alternate scenarios that didn't even make sense. *Maybe Ginger Spice isn't leaving the group. Maybe she's leaving the soup! Who wants soup, anyway?!? Or maybe she's sleeving the group! They do show their arms a lot! Ginger's believing the poop? What the hell was going on?!?*

"While Halliwell is choosing to pursue solo projects," the anchor continued, "the rest of the Spice Girls have confirmed that they will continue on without her for the remainder of their Spice World US tour . . ."

Then the big, giant, calloused man hand of reality slapped me in the face and reality sank in. Tears began falling down my cheeks, dripping into my family-sized bag of Funyuns, taking the "fun" right out of them. I was about to snap. To Ginger Snap, if you will.

In a daze, I stumbled to my dresser, opened my underwear drawer—the place where I kept all my "treasures" for safekeeping—and grabbed my ticket to the upcoming concert, clutching it to my now-broken heart. How could this be happening? The Spice Girls without Ginger? That was like Mount Rushmore without Lincoln, Disney without Mickey, *Family Matters* without Urkle.

As I stared at my ticket with the words "NO REFUNDS" printed boldly at the top, my disappointment started to mutate into anger. How dare my favorite Spice Girl pull out of the tour right before the fateful concert that I was convinced would result in us becoming best friends and music industry colleagues!? I looked across the room at the Spice Girls poster on my wall, and Ginger's smiling face looked back at me, mocking the betrayal I felt, her two fingers making a now oh-so-ironic peace sign. Okay, now I was furious. Peace? Honey, this was WAR!

Suddenly, Ginger left a bad taste in my mouth. I walked straight to my Spice Girls memorabilia shelf, grabbed the Ginger doll (still in the box, of course), and stared at her, seeing her with new eyes—eyes that were now brimming with tears. Her Union Jack dress now a loud red, white, and blue reminder that she had shattered *our* union! The once-glamorous streak of blond in her hair now a brassy symbol of her recently revealed streak of cruelty! Her platform sneakers now seeming extra sneaky! I turned the doll toward the wall. I couldn't even look at her—she knew what she had done. You guys, I couldn't even eat gingerbread cookies anymore. That's how bad it got.

That next week was a blur. As with any big, sudden breakup, my head was full of questions: *Why did she leave? Why did she do this to me? Why does God hate me?* And more importantly, would they do the concert with just four girls or try to replace her with some lackluster fill-in? And would that replacement be dressed as Ginger or have her own persona? And what would her name be? Phony Spice? Secret Spice? I mean, it worked for KFC (I still couldn't tell you what they use in that sweet, sweet bucket o' drumsticks).

After a few days, my anger faded a bit. Despite feeling that, legally, I was entitled to at least a partial refund of my hard-earned money, I decided to stop focusing on the negative and make the most of this concert experience. After all, I still had four friends I needed to support—Posh, Scary, Sporty, and Baby. They needed me, too. God, looking back, I was so selfless.

Bravely, I gathered my strength and somehow managed to enjoy the concert. I just let go of everything and allowed myself to be swept away by the music and the energy. But every so often, when I least expected it, I felt an emptiness—the void left by Ginger. But then I shook it off, sang along, and nailed the choreography from our seats in the nosebleed section. From all the way up here, everything seemed so small—even my problems.

After the concert, I slowly forgot about it all and moved on, just like I do with every exercise program I've ever started. Life got busy and I put my drama with Ginger Spice on the shelf—the spice shelf, if you will. Years later, usually after a few drinks at happy hour when a Spice Girls song played at a bar—now considered "retro '90s music" by millennials—I'd fantasize about coming face-to-face with Ginger and telling her the story of when she crushed my teen dreams. I would really give her a piece of my mind! But then the song would end and so would the daydream and I would be left with the truth: The chances of me crossing paths with Ginger—or *any* of the Spice Girls, for that matter— were long gone.

And just like that time I bought all that stock in Myspace, boy, was I wrong.

Flash-forward to the 2012 Summer Olympics in London. No, I wasn't competing. Turns out they don't have Olympic events called "Channel Surfing" or "*Steel Magnolias* Quote-athon"— yet. I had just covered the games for E! and was on my way back to Los Angeles. One of the best parts of working in TV—along with the free food at the craft services table and swag bags full of complimentary hair products—is flying first class.

Honey, let me tell you, first-class is where it's at! We're talking free-flowing champagne, big comfy seats, and warm nuts. I'm a real sucker for a warm nut! And I think it's especially cruel the way the flight attendants open that curtain separating first class from economy the moment the freshly baked chocolate chip cookies come out of the oven. Trust me, when I book my own flights, I'm back in coach smelling those cookies and cursing those elitist first-class a-holes. But right now, thanks to E! I was one of them. My wish for all you reading this right now is that one day, ideally on someone else's dime, you can be one of those a-holes, too!

As I was getting all cozy in my enormous, butter-soft leather seat that, like something out of *Transformers*, would magically morph into a bed later in the flight, somewhere over the Atlantic Ocean, I saw Her. She was sauntering down the aisle in impossibly high stiletto heels—the super-expensive ones with the fancy red bottoms. She was in head-to-toe black: skintight leather pants and a structured dominatrix jacket with the collar flipped up, framing her world-famous face and even worlder-famouser asymmetric hairstyle. (I can almost hear you screaming at me, "Ross, who was this mysterious woman!?" Simmer down, the "reveal" is coming . . . I was trying to build suspense, silly.) IT WAS VICTORIA "POSH SPICE" BECKHAM!

Before I could catch my breath, Posh walked past me, with her youngest baby, Harper, and her nanny, a modern-day Mary Poppins. I subtly twisted around to see where they'd be sitting and—OMG—they sat directly behind me!

I, of course, being the show business professional that I am, treated the whole thing like it was no biggie, totally kept my cool, and went back to my *Us Weekly*. Just kidding! In a frenzy, I clumsily fumbled for my iPhone that was charging next to me (yep, first class has outlets!), and blatantly tweeted "OMG, you guys, Posh Spice is sitting directly behind me on my flight home to LA!"

Her unquestionable glamour instantly made *me* feel more glamorous just by my mere proximity. I was now officially what I call GA: Glamour-Adjacent! And I didn't think it was too much to ask the Universe for maybe just one little memorable interaction with Posh Spice. Nothing major, mind you. I'd never be pushy with Poshy. We'd just be two beautiful people giving a smile or a wave on the way to the restroom or a subtle nod that silently acknowledged, "I ordered the Southwestern chicken breast for lunch, too!"

But then I realized something depressing. The plane was about to take off, and if she was anything like me, and of course

Posh Spice was *just* like me (I mean we both ordered the South-western chicken, hello!), the moment we were in the air she was going to put on some headphones, slip on a matching, vaguely S&M-looking sleep mask, and go "off grid." Dammit, just my luck. Now we'd never be besties.

Just then, as if on cue, I heard the voice of the captain over the PA system informing us of a delay. "Unfortunately, we're gonna have a bit of a wait here on the tarmac, folks. So just sit back and relax for a while."

Wait, what's that sound? Oh yeah: opportunity knocking! But how could I possibly say hello? I mean, it was Victoria Freakin' Beckham and she was *behind* me. So I decided to just give her some space and use this time to go back on Twitter. Suddenly I experienced some major turbulence, and the plane hadn't even taken off! I felt my stomach doing somersaults. Why? Because since posting my innocent, harmless "Posh is on my plane" tweet, dozens of people had taken it upon themselves to tweet at her about me! "Hey @VictoriaBeckham, say hi to @HelloRoss! He's in the seat in front of you!"

Damn those nosy people! God bless those nosy people!

I immediately felt a mash-up of exhilaration and panic. Convinced I was freaking out about nothing, I snuck a peek and saw—you guessed it—Posh on her phone. Okay, but what were the chances a big star like her was checking her Twitter? I would guess about the same as the odds of me being hired to join the all-male strip show Thunder from Down Under in Vegas. I'm not even Australian. Chippendales maybe, but Thunder from Down Under? *No, don't be ridiculous. Ain't gonna happen, Ross. Enjoy your champagne and your warm nuts and just simmer the fuck down, you delusional drama queen.*

Just then I feel a *tap tap tap* on my shoulder. Let me tell you something, I've been tapped on the shoulder a lot (everything from "Pardon me, but aren't you that super-Gay guy with the super-Gay voice from that super-Gay show?" to "Excuse me, sir, but can you please crunch the celery from your Bloody Mary a little quieter? This is a *library*"), and this was the most sophisticated and nuanced tap I had ever experienced.

Call it gut instinct, but I could tell it was my soon-to-be-favorite Spice Girl, Posh. To be fair, I was pretty sure it wasn't the nanny, and it certainly wasn't the baby, so that pretty much left just one Posh-ibility as to who was behind me tapping me on the shoulder. I was afraid to turn around, but I did. It was Her, and in the most delicious British accent she said, "Hello there! I see you tweeted about me." Her voice and attitude were so casual and friendly that my nervousness immediately melted away and we totally hit it off, like a super-successful internet date—one of the really good ones that don't end up being reenacted on *Forensic Files*.

We talked for a long time, and what struck me was how funny she was. I'm always surprised when beautiful people are funny. It doesn't seem fair, right? But she was both—like a soft-serve swirl cone of perfection—and we just talked and talked and talked. Then, just as she was laughing at a particularly witty thing I had said, the captain informed us that we were ready to take off, his voice bringing this part of my fairy tale to an end, not unlike the clock striking midnight in *Cinderella*. But I wasn't worried. I knew that all fairy tales ended "happily ever after," and this one would be no different.

Once in the air, even with the seatbelt sign still illuminated (Fun Fact: famous people don't follow rules), my new soul mate, Victoria, or as I now call her, Vicki, ducked into the first-class lavatory to pull what I can only describe as a "reverse Superman." You see, she entered looking like a chic Posh Spice superhero and emerged the yoga mom equivalent to Clark Kent in a pair of Uggs, comfortable stretch pants, and a long, roomy sweater.

We talked on and off the entire twelve-hour flight. I'll admit, during one of our conversations, I was tempted to bring up the whole GingerGate 1998 thing. I was still upset about it, but I realized that this wasn't the time or the place. At one point, I fell asleep. When I awoke, I couldn't help but worry that maybe I had been snoring. Or even worse, drooling! But then I thought, *You know what? Friends accept each other the way they are. Relax.*

When we were about to land, she once again disappeared into the restroom and changed back into the stylish and catlike Posh Spice the world knew and loved. And then she put the cherry on top of the sexy superstar sundae: a pair of big, black expensive designer sunglasses that simultaneously screamed "Look at me / Don't look at me!"

She had been so cool and funny and nice on the flight that I had kinda forgotten who she was for a brief moment. That is until we got off the plane and walked to baggage claim, where she was immediately surrounded by a swarm of relentless paparazzi screaming her name.

Thank God she was on my flight. Not only so we could share that magical moment but had she not been there that day it could have easily been me ruthlessly harassed by the paparazzi! I find it's nearly impossible to escape them, especially when I'm standing on a bench near baggage claim, waving my arms, loudly begging them, "Hey, over here! It's me, Ross Mathews from TV! Pleeeease respect my privacy!"

If you think that's the end of my Spice Girls story, you can

"Stop right now, thank you very much." My connection to the Spice Girls isn't over yet.

Cut to November of 2013. I was hosting the first season of my E! TV show, *Hello Ross!* My guest that week was none other than Scary Spice herself, Mel B. She was currently a judge on *America's Got Talent* and was promoting the new season. She could have been promoting root canal and I would have had her on as a guest! But I also knew that if I was going to have the Spice Girls on my show, on my couch, I was going to get something off my chest. I hadn't forgotten what had gone down way back in 1998 when Ginger all but ruined my life by quitting the group.

Something had to be said. I needed closure. I had missed my opportunity on that flight with Posh, and I knew the chances of being face-to-face with another Spice Girl were slim. I mean, what are the odds of me ever running into Sporty Spice at Dick's Sporting Goods or Baby Spice at Baby Gap? Not good. Trust me, I've hung out at both for hours and hours, day after day, and *nothing!*

Mel B was a delight. She was easy to book on the show and nice to everyone on our staff, so I felt like I could really go there with her. As our interview was wrapping up, after I had already asked about the new season of her show and her newly released single, I decided to go rogue. Despite years of intensive therapy, what had happened with Ginger was still eating at me. This was my last chance and I wasn't going to miss it. In front of our entire studio audience, I said, "I need to talk to you about something else. I have a bone to pick with you."

She looked confused. I continued, telling her the story of how Ginger had quit the band after I had already purchased tickets.

"So," I said seriously, looking her dead in the eye and holding out my hand, "I'd like one-fifth of my money back."

Without missing a nineties pop beat, Mel B got up and walked off the set. The audience gasped and I thought to myself, *Oh no, I've finally done it. I have crossed the line. Sweet li'l ol' me has taken things too far and upset a guest so much that they have actually just stormed off the set of my talk show! First Ginger leaves the band and then I force Mel B to leave my show? This is a scandal!* Scary Spice was scaring the shit out of me. Suddenly, she walked back on set with a big smile on her face with her cell phone in her hand, saying, "Let's call her! Let's call Miss Geri Halliwell!"

From 1998 to 2013 the tension had been building. Now was my opportunity to tell Ginger Spice how I really felt. As she made that fateful call I tried to look at Ginger's number on Scary's phone screen and commit it to memory. Ring . . . *I can't believe this is finally happening.* Ring . . . *This is my big chance.* Ring . . . *Let's do this, Mathews.*

The following is a transcript of exactly what happened. Feel free to act it out with your friends. Toss a coin or draw straws as to who gets to play Ginger.

GINGER SPICE: Hello?

(AUDIENCE GASPS)

ROSS: Oh, my God, this is Ross, is this—AHHHHH!

(LAUGHTER)

GINGER SPICE: Hello, Ross!

ROSS: Hello . . . Ummm . . . Oh, my God, what do I call you? Geri? Ginger? Geri?

GINGER SPICE: Hi, Ross, how are you?

ROSS: Like, really good. I'm really good.

SCARY SPICE: Ross has a bone to pick with you and us
 because—

ROSS: Well, maybe I'm changing my mind!

(AUDIENCE CHEERS, SCARY AND GINGER LAUGH)

ROSS: Never mind: I forgive you and I love you!

(APPLAUSE)

(END SCENE)

Of course the moment I heard Ginger's voice, all my bit-terness and lust for revenge went right out the window. All was forgiven. I wish I had a time machine to go back to 1998 and tell teenage Ross to simmer the fuck down just a little bit. He may not have gotten to see Ginger in concert back then, but one day our paths would cross in the most unusual of ways.

The Universe always has a plan—it will bring two people together if they're meant to be. The Spice Girls taught me how to embrace my uniqueness, my unicorn realness. And more im-portantly, they taught me how to forgive. And that's how, when it comes to friendship—real or imagined—"2 Become 1."

CHAPTER EIGHT

The Kardashian/Jenner Story

COCKTAIL

Kardashian Kamikaze

½ ounce vodka

½ ounce lime juice

½ ounce triple sec

Combine all ingredients into a shaker with ice. Shake it harder than Kim shakes her booty to Kanye's newest single. Strain into a glass and garnish with a lime peel.

Korndashians with a Kick!

1 tablespoon unsalted butter

Corn—either 4 cobs of freshly cut corn or 1 bag of frozen corn
(either works great!)

3 tablespoons mayonnaise

3 ounces cotija cheese (or feta if you can't find cotija),
crumbled

1 teaspoon paprika

Salt and pepper, to taste

Chives

1 large lime

Melt butter in a pan and sauté corn on medium/low for about 10 minutes, or until it begins to brown slightly. Stir often. Once cooked, place into a large serving bowl and mix in mayonnaise, cheese, paprika, salt, and pepper. Sprinkle chopped chives over the top and squeeze the entire lime over it all. Delish!

FULL DISCLOSURE: I like the Kardashians. There, I said it. I know, I know—lots of people are annoyed by them, and I get it. They're everywhere, they're polarizing, and they're richer than . . . all of us combined. And I can understand why some people might be jealous of their seemingly effortless success and over-the-top lavish lifestyle. But whenever I've kept up with the Kardashians, I've always found the entire family to be kind, warm, funny, and smarter than most people give them credit for.

I first met the Kardashians around 2007 when their now-infamous reality TV juggernaut was launching on E! This was around the time *Chelsea Lately* was becoming a hit on the same network, and I was fortunate to be a part of its early roundtable of comics. These frequent appearances on *Chelsea* eventually led to me joining the E! red carpet team, alongside Ryan Seacrest, Giuliana Rancic, and Kelly Osbourne.

Sometimes in life, you have no way of knowing how a certain thing works until you experience it for yourself. Like how to eat an artichoke, how to put on Spanx, or how to smoothly pretend like you're talking on the phone when the lady in the car next to you catches you singing along with Katy Perry at the top of your lungs. You know, the really important stuff.

Well, here's something else I never knew until it happened to me: When you're on a hit show on a popular TV network, you immediately become part of a big extended family, spending quality time together at promotional events, rubbing elbows at cocktail parties, and hoarding gift bags at premieres. And, just like with other families, everyone has their role: The snarky dry "uncle" was *The Soup's* Joel McHale; our hilarious "aunt" was the late great Joan Rivers of *Fashion Police*; and the Kardashians were the "Kool Kousins." And me? I guess I was sort of the quirky, gay pink sheep of the family (not that that's a "b'aaaaaaaaaaad" thing).

Now remember, this was in the infancy of the *Keeping Up with the Kardashians* franchise, prior to when it became a full-fledged cultural phenomenon. Way before Kim's world-famous ass broke the internet, way before Khloé's *Revenge Body*, and way before Caitlyn Jenner made her transition (can you believe she doesn't spell it with a "K"? What a rebel!).

I'll never forget the first time I really bonded with Kris, the girls' mother/manager, a combo now commonly known as a "momager." (Side note: I just typed the word "momager" for the first time on my laptop and was surprised to see no squiggly red line underneath it. Do you know what that means? It's a real word! Now *that's* the power of Kris Jenner.)

My friend Lara Spencer was hosting *The Insider* around this time and invited Kris and myself out to dinner at Dan Tana's, the legendary West Hollywood Italian eatery where celebrities often go to cut loose by actually consuming a carb or two. For one night only, it was pasta instead of Pilates, hot bread instead of hot yoga, spaghetti instead of spin class. Or, for me, just a normal weeknight.

Dan Tana's turned out to be the perfect setting to get to know Kris. Just like the popular restaurant, she was somehow ritzy yet rustic, glamorous yet grounded, dazzling yet down to earth. What struck me most was just how nurturing and maternal she was. Much more *mom* than *manager*.

Thanks to the chianti and the casual conversation, everything seemed very comfortably normal—just a few new friends bonding over dinner. That is, until the door swung open and Kim and Kourtney breezed into the restaurant with a lightning storm of blinding paparazzi cameras flashing behind them, illuminating the darkened dining room. *Whoa*, I thought. That's when I realized these women were going to be huge—even bigger than the Buick-sized chunk of Dan Tana's famous lasagna I had just devoured.

And I was right. Faster than you could say "laser hair removal," the Kardashians became the biggest stars on TV and pop culture at large, raking in tens of millions of dollars and dating every NBA player I've ever heard of (and to be fair, I've only heard of them because they dated a Kardashian. My love of football does not, sadly, extend to the world of basketball, and that's just how the ball bounces). As a result, they became an easy target for comedians. They even became a regular topic on *Chelsea Lately*, although I personally had made the decision to never make a mean-spirited joke about them or throw them under the bus. I never really made jokes like that about anyone, actually, let alone people I considered friends. That's just not my kind of humor. But, to be fair, if Chelsea or one of the comics on the roundtable got in a good zinger at the Kardashians' expense, sometimes I couldn't help but laugh. I mean, funny is funny, right?

The Kardashians became so successful that every time I saw Kris or the girls after that, I have to be honest, I got a little nervous. It's weird when friends suddenly become super-famous. I've experienced it a few times and I always react the same way. I find myself getting very hyper-aware and self-conscious of my behavior. I never want that famous friend to feel like I want something from them, like so many others do. So, rather than just "being," I start overcompensating and second-guessing everything I say and do.

When the Kardashians became a household name, they were still the same people they'd always been (other than the hair extensions and brand-spankin'-new lips), but I began having a hard time separating the real them from the reality TV them. Does that make sense? So in order to subtly assure them that all I wanted from them was their friendship, I tried to play it cool.

It turns out I played it a little too cool.

Fast-forward to the summer of 2012. Both *Keeping Up with*

the Kardashians and *Chelsea Lately* were bigger than ever and *E! News* asked me to travel to the Summer Olympics in London as a special correspondent.

You know, it literally just occurred to me that for a chubby kid who always preferred home ec to PE, I sure have been to a lot of Olympics in my life: Salt Lake City, Torino, and London. There's nothing like covering the Olympics—you're in the epicenter of excitement and literally the entire world is watching. Whether for *The Tonight Show* or *E! News*, it's always fun to cover these games in my own silly way. Honey, if they gave out gold medals for making bad sports puns and gushing over Spandex-clad athletes, I'd make Michael Phelps look like a slacker!

The other special correspondent for *E! News* in London that year was none other than Kardashian patriarch and Olympic legend Caitlyn Jenner. This, of course, was before Caitlyn courageously transitioned and told us her new name. She was still presenting as male at the time, but for this story I'll use the name Caitlyn and "she" pronouns because I checked with my friends at GLAAD—the Gay and Lesbian Alliance Against Defamation—and they guided me on how to be most respectful to Caitlyn and the entire transgender community.

Caitlyn and I weren't what you'd call close. We'd met many times at events, and I'd interviewed her on red carpets, but she wasn't one to come giggle at happy hour with us. Nevertheless, I was excited to get a chance to get to know her better. I mean, we're talking about an Olympic and cultural icon who had been on a Wheaties box. (Granted, I prefer Lucky Charms—sorry, but Wheaties don't even have mini marshmallows. You call that cereal?) And as if that wasn't enough, Caitlyn had helped raise the most successful and exciting showbiz siblings since Hanson.

What? Sorry, but "MMMBop" is a totally underrated MMMMasterpiece!

Caitlyn was very nice, though somewhat distant. But she was also actually very funny in a grumpy kind of way, sort of like a curmudgeon, a word that always makes me crave a turducken (a chicken inside a duck inside a turkey) or a CroMuffin (that trendy new bakery mash-up of a croissant and a muffin—okay, I made that last one up, but it's a good idea, right?).

The first time Caitlyn saw me in London, she said, "Oh, there's Ross! Just living life the way he wants to live it!"

I remember being confused by that, almost as if it was an accusation. *What could possibly be wrong with living life the way you want to live it?* Of course, looking back, it makes sense. After all, this was coming from someone who, at the time, maybe wasn't living life the way they wanted to. But at that moment I just brushed it off.

One afternoon, as Caitlyn and I were walking through the Olympic Village on our way to the *E! News* set, I overheard her talking on her cell phone. "Okay, Kris, sounds good . . ."

I interjected, "Is that Kris? Tell her I said hi!"

Caitlyn continued her conversation, as if she hadn't heard me. "Okay, talk to you later."

"Tell her I said hello!" I repeated, shouting way too loudly.

"Bye-bye." Caitlyn hung up.

Hmmm, I thought. *What was that about?* But I let it go, adding, "Next time you talk to Kris, please tell her hi for me!"

Caitlyn shook her head, slipping her cell phone into her pants pocket. "I don't think that would be a good idea. She told me not to talk to you."

Huh?

Now, if we were on a reality TV show, this would totally be when they cut to a commercial for one of those pillows that make you stop snoring or that yogurt that helps you poop. You know, the oh-so-dramatic, we-need-a-cliffhanger-so-people-don't-change-the-channel moment of the show? Except this wasn't reality TV, it was real life.

I was dumbfounded. "Wait, are you kidding?"

She wasn't kidding. "Nope. I think she's mad at you."

"Oh, my God! What?!?" I didn't understand. Here's something you need to know about your good friend Ross Mathews: I don't do well when people are mad at me. I always feel the need to fix it immediately.

Caitlyn shrugged her shoulders. "You'll have to ask Kris."

"Call her back!" I heard myself uncharacteristically yelling at the Olympic legend standing in front of me. Caitlyn took out her phone and dialed. "Kris, someone needs to talk to you."

She handed me her phone. "Kris? It's Ross. Are you mad at me?"

She didn't pull any punches. "Well, Ross, I honestly felt like you've been distant. Plus, I know you're on *Chelsea Lately*, and I think that show can be very mean to us sometimes. I just assumed you had kind of turned on us."

I got what she meant right away. Suddenly I saw the situation through *her* eyes. I pictured her watching me on *Chelsea Lately* as I laughed uproariously at snarky jokes about her daughters. Remember when I said Kris was much more *mom* than *manager*? Well, someone was messing with her Kubs, and we had obviously unleashed the protective Mama Lion within!

I tried to explain. "Oh, Kris, I'm sorry. I promise you I've never made a mean joke about the family. I wouldn't do that. First of all, I love you all, and second, 'mean' isn't how I roll—on or off camera. And as far as me seeming distant? The absolute truth is that you all just got so super-famous that I guess I just got super-nervous. I'm so sorry if my nerves came across as anything other than that. I adore you."

Kris seemed relieved. "I'm so happy to hear that! I was so sad to think that maybe we weren't friends anymore!"

I was relieved, too. "Happy hour ASAP!"

"Deal!"

And as soon as I got back from London, Kris and I met up for happy hour. It was like nothing had ever happened. Same ol' Kris—dishing up really great gossip and even better advice. Soon after that, we flew together on a private jet to New York City for an E! event. I remember laughing so hard when Kris—a former flight attendant—got up and served everyone drinks during the flight. "Here's your vodka soda with two limes, sir! Can I get you anything else?"

Being back in Kris's good graces didn't just mean that I got my friend back. It also meant that I was invited to the family's famous Christmas Eve party. And girl, trust me—this holiday party puts every other holiday party to shame. Superstars at every table, holiday decorations that would make Disneyland look like a trailer park, and most importantly, a Christmas dinner buffet that would blow your mind—and your waistband!

Oh, and as each guest left the party every year, Kris made sure everybody got a gift. One year the gift was a crystal bowl, another year it was a pizza oven—*A PIZZA OVEN!* But my favorite gift was a beautiful set of silverware inside a giant silver egg. It was valued at more than $3,700. How do I know it cost that much? 'Cuz bitch you better believe I Googled the price when I got home!

Don't judge: You'd do it, too! Yep, almost four grand. My first car didn't even cost that much. It was a used Chevy Citation that I bought for $600 from a guy in a trailer park. Every time a policeman pulled me over and said he was going to have to give me a citation, I would point at the name of the car and say, "But look, I've already got a Citation, Officer!" (I always got a ticket.)

It was at one of these Christmas Eve parties where I first saw Caitlyn after her transition. This was right after her public transition and groundbreaking interview with Diane Sawyer. Caitlyn seemed much lighter and happier than she did when she was still presenting as male. She was glowing even brighter than the thousands of Christmas lights artfully strewn throughout the backyard. Reflecting on what she had said to me in London all those years earlier (that somewhat cryptic "Oh, there's Ross! Just living life the way he wants to live it!"), I felt the need to open up to her.

"Caitlyn, I wish I would've known. I could have been an ally for you."

"Ross," she said, smiling like I'd never seen her smile before, "I couldn't even be honest with myself."

"Well," I said, quoting her back to herself, "it's just good to see you living life the way you want to live it."

I could tell she got the reference. We both chuckled and hugged. And then I made a mad dash to get in line at the buffet. Again. They were still serving food, and you best believe I will elbow a bitch for some honeybaked ham!

CHAPTER NINE

The Celine Dion Story

COCKTAIL

French Canadian 75

2 ounces dry gin

¾ ounce fresh lemon juice

¾ ounce simple syrup (equal parts sugar and water, heated
    until dissolved)

2 ounces champagne

1 lemon

Mix gin, lemon juice, and simple syrup and pour over ice. Then
add champagne to the top, garnish with lemon peel, and sing the
Canadian national anthem in French.

ROSSIPE

My Artichoke Heart Will Go On

2 large artichokes

Olive oil

Salt and pepper, to taste

1 whole lemon

Mayonnaise

Garlic chili sauce

Cut artichokes in half and boil in salted water until you can easily stick a knife into the stem. Then brush the insides with olive oil, sprinkle with salt and pepper, and grill (open side down) on a BBQ or in a pan. Once they're seared and/or slightly charred, squeeze half a lemon over them and serve with garlic chili dipping sauce.

Dipping sauce: Combine 3 parts mayonnaise with 1 part garlic chili sauce (located in the Asian foods section of any grocery store). Squeeze the other half of the lemon in the bowl and add salt/pepper to taste.

I HAVE A confession to make. Are you sitting? Okay, here we go. I never really "got" Celine Dion. I'm sorry! Back in the day, I would watch her on TV singing while constantly beating her chest—I mean, who does that?—and think, *What is wrong with her?* She was just too much, even for me. And I still can't figure out why she wore that backwards white tuxedo on the Oscars red carpet. Am I the only one who couldn't tell if she was coming or going?

I know—the status of my Gay Card should be downgraded from Platinum to Bronze, right? But don't worry. I eventually came around. The year was 2002 and I had just graduated from college. I was already on *The Tonight Show* but, like most recent college graduates, was still struggling financially and trying to figure out what I was going to do with the rest of my life. It was a weird time for me—everywhere I went, I was recognized by people who had seen me on TV, but I hadn't landed a contract yet, so I was barely making enough money to pay the $600 rent for my tiny Los Angeles apartment in the worst part of town. I certainly didn't have any extra money to do anything fun.

So when the people from LA's big Top 40 radio station, 102.7 KIIS FM, reached out and asked if I wanted to attend their big annual Wango Tango music festival and concert at the Rose Bowl in Pasadena, I said yes faster than you can say "Does it by any chance also include free food and an open bar?"

That year, Wango Tango featured iconic acts like Jessica Simpson, O-Town, Jennifer Love Hewitt, Nick Carter—you know, artists who have really stood the test of time. The big headliner, though, was Ms. Dion. The irony here is that when I heard she was set to perform, I literally rolled my eyes. *Ugh,* I thought, *I'll stay to listen to O-Town's "Liquid Dreams," but I'll go to the bathroom when Celine hits the stage and no doubt her chest again.*

What a fool I was! The moment she walked on stage, I stood up to leave for my preplanned bathroom trip and to maybe splurge on a churro. And then, as if on cue, Celine opened her mouth, and what came out stopped me dead in my tracks. Suddenly I no longer had to pee, nor did I have a hankering for that deep-fried, cinnamon, sugar-dusted delicacy. I stood there dumbfounded, slack-jawed, gobsmacked, as a sound like I'd never heard before echoed throughout the Rose Bowl. The voice of an angel. Pure. Original. Strong. THE REAL DEAL.

I was shook. You guys, she was so good. "A New Day Has Come."

On the drive home, I stopped by the music store to buy all her CDs (just typing that makes me feel like a fucking dinosaur) and began my education in Celine 101. I couldn't believe I had wasted so much time being distracted by her signature chest-bumping, incoherent rambling when she talked to the audience, and awkward French Canadian humor. Who cared? With a voice like that, I didn't care if she did Pilates on stage! She was a gift to humankind!

After listening to her entire music catalog, I was obsessed. Maybe when you sing as passionately as she did and with such gusto, your heart has a tendency to momentarily stop beating and you have to fist-bump your own chest to start it back up again? Whatever the reason, I let it go and even embraced her frequent and violent self-beatings.

I knew I had to see her perform live again, and this time I wanted—no, *needed*—a whole concert. Cut to September of 2015. "It's All Coming Back to Me Now." Celine had a residency at Caesars Palace in Las Vegas and there was no way I was missing it. Now, I'm gonna get real real with you about something and—warning—it's gonna sound like I'm one of "those" people. It's gonna sound tacky and opportunistic and douchey. And it is. But let me explain . . .

Even at my level of "fame," it's necessary to have a team of people around me making sure everything about Ross Mathews Industries works smoothly. I have an assistant, an agent, a manager, a lawyer, an accountant, and a publicist. As the hunky construction worker in the Village People once said, "It takes a village, people." Or was that Hillary Clinton? Either way, it's true.

As I was online one night Googling "affordable Celine Dion tickets," something occurred to me. *You have a publicist, dumdum,* I thought. *Why not ask her to see if she can get you free tickets? Famous people do that all the time. Why shouldn't you at least try? The only risk is that you're not famous enough to be on Team Dion's radar. Big deal!*

So I emailed my publicist asking for two tickets. What? I didn't wanna go "All By Myself"!

If there's one thing that I have learned from nearly two decades in show business—other than don't make eye contact with Madonna—is that you have to ask for what you want. No one is going to rub your feet or remove the yellow M&M's from that enormous bowl in your dressing room if you don't ask them to. I'm totally kidding, honey. I like all colors of M&M's.

To my utter surprise, my publicist emailed back the next day. "Celine's people would love to give you tickets to come see the show and come backstage to take a picture with Celine!"

OMG. FREE SEATS? A MEET AND GREET?!? This was better than I ever could've imagined!

How had this happened? What was the process? I pictured Celine sitting with her team at her diamond desk in her twenty-four-karat-gold office looking at a list of celebrity requests and either approving them or denying them free tickets.

"The president? No!" she'd exclaim in her French Canadian accent while crossing his name off the list and once again dramatically thumping her chest (ouch!). "The first man on the moon? No! Wendy the Snapple Lady? Is she even a thing anymore? Hell no!" Then she'd get to my name. "Ross Mathews? That pudgy gay with the lady voice? Oh! I love him! Yes! I insist that he see my show and come backstage to meet me! As sure as my name is Celine Dion, I demand to meet Ross Mathews! Bring him to me!"

This was going to be as big for her as it was for me. I was about to be in a picture with Celine Dion! It was going to look like the poster for *Beauty and the Beast*, but with two beauties and no beast.

So it was off to Las Vegas I went. "I Drove All Night." Actually, that's not true—I took a forty-five-minute flight from Burbank, but she doesn't have a song called "Forty-Five-Minute Flight from Burbank." (Although, if she did, I'm sure it'd be a hit. Celine, if you're reading this—write that song!)

I brought my best friend Taya with me and we were both on pins and needles. I mean, hello! We were about to meet the actual Celine Dion! I'll be honest with you—we even stopped for a couple drinks before the show. I needed it. I'm not a professional, but I'm pretty sure even Dr. Quinn, Medicine Woman, would prescribe two glasses of champagne for a moment like this. "Take two and call me in the morning—with all the juicy details!"

Once we got to Caesars Palace, I texted my contact at Team Dion. She got back right away. "Get in the VIP line and I'll be right out to grab you." VIP? This was going to ruin me for all other concerts.

We lined up behind about thirty other people. Full disclosure: There aren't many things I will stand in line for . . . Cronuts, several free Costco samples of boneless buffalo wings, and meeting Celine Dion. That's about it.

To say I was nervous is like saying *Magic Mike* is just an okay movie. And just like the very first time I saw *Magic Mike*, my palms were now sweating, and all sorts of exciting but terrifying feelings were vibrating throughout my body. I can only imagine that this is what it's like when you're meeting the Queen of England. Do you curtsy? Look at her feet and bend at the waist? If you try to shake her hand, will you immediately be tackled by two beefy security guards right out of *Men in Black* and be wrestled to the ground?

Before I could spend any more time overanalyzing it all, the lady from Team Dion came out. "Okay, VIPs, please come this way." Then she came up to me. "Ross! It's so great to meet you! We're all so excited you're here."

We? WE?!? WE are so excited?!? Who did she mean? Her and her gay assistant? Her and the security guard at the door? Surely she couldn't possibly mean her and the one and only Celine Dion. OMG. Maybe Celine actually did know who I was! My mind was running wild. Would she bring me up on stage and sing to me? If so, did she take requests? I'm not gonna be picky, but I'd really love "The Power of Love," but if she wants to do the equally appropriate "When I Need You," while staring into my adoring eyes, that would be cool, too.

The thirty other VIPs were escorted along with my bestie Taya and me into a hidden back area about the size of a doctor's waiting room, which seemed appropriate because I was about to have a heart attack. *This is nice,* I thought. Just then, the lady from Team Dion said, "Okay, everybody wait here. Ross, you two can come with me."

This was getting so good!!!

We were plucked from the others and brought down a deep, dark hallway that led to a glowing soft light. This dark void with a light at the end of a tunnel made me briefly wonder whether I had actually died of a heart attack and was now crossing over to the other side. It turned out I was still very much alive—perhaps more alive than I had felt in years. I could feel a tangible electricity in the air. No, I wasn't dead, but I had traveled to heaven: a hidden room bathed in the most flattering lighting I had ever seen. This secret chamber was exactly 68.5 degrees and filled with what seemed like three thousand roses. The assistant gave us instructions. "Stand right on that mark on the floor and Ms. Dion will be here momentarily."

It was just me, Taya, the roses, and a man with a camera. Then I heard the unmistakable "clip-clop" of expensive high heels coming down a hallway and suddenly a door opened. There she was: Celine Dion, looking absolutely gorgeous. Her hair flowing, her skin glowing. She looked up as she walked toward me. *What's she gonna say? What do I say? Should I bring up the weather? Politics? Maybe dinner after the show?* But before I could say anything, Celine took the reins.

Without making eye contact with either of us, she casually chirped, "Hi, folks!"

Like clockwork, she abruptly took her mark between the two of us and looked up at the man with the camera and smiled her dazzling smile. *Click.* Then Celine clapped her hands, turned around, and said as she walked away, "Enjoy the show!"

And that was it. It was like the first time I had sex—an eternity of anticipation and excitement followed by three seconds of awkward bliss and an anticlimactic ending. And I was thrilled (both times)!

Look—I don't need to be Celine Dion's best friend. And not every celebrity story is going to end like a fairy tale where the famous person and I end up bonding and staying in touch forever and ever. I got a picture with a legend and I couldn't be happier.

In the photo we took that day, you can see how excited I was to meet her. Celine gave me that moment. She didn't have to do that. And right after that, at her show, as I sat in my free front-row seats, she gave me the chills. What else could a boy want? And "That's the Way It Is."

CHAPTER TEN

The *Big Brother* Story

COCKTAIL

Omarosa Mimosa

2 blood oranges

1 expensive bottle of champagne

Juice the blood oranges and mix 1 part juice with 2 parts champagne. Drink two glasses by yourself and then practice your best "villain" face in the mirror. Then finish the entire bottle. Invite a friend (if you can really trust them).

RealiTV Dinner

Girl, heat up a Hungry-Man! You've got too much shit TV to watch!

WITH ALMOST TWENTY years of show business experience under my BeDazzled belt buckle, I've been asked to be on more than my fair share of reality shows. And to my credit—or my stupidity—I've turned most of them down. Here's just a sampling:

- Food Network's *Worst Cooks in America: Celebrity Edition*? Sorry, honey, but I cook every day. Hello, haven't you heard of my trademarked and tasty Rossipes?

- NBC's *Celebrity Apprentice*? Sweetie, I don't think so. Now that he's in the White House, technically Trump works for me, not the other way around.

- CBS's *The Amazing Race*? No way, José. That show gives me far too much anxiety and motion sickness. My idea of an "amazing race" is frantically running through the aisles of Trader Joe's when I get there five minutes before closing time to do a week's worth of grocery shopping.

- ABC's *Dancing with the Stars*? Although I did attend a meeting with network bigwigs regarding my being a contestant, technically they never asked me. But I probably would've said no to them, too. Despite what I assume are your fantasies about me, I'm afraid that when it comes to dancing, I'm more Fred Flintstone than Fred Astaire. I can't do the fox-trot or the samba or the tango. And let's be honest, the only salsa in my life is piled on a tortilla chip and is of the chunky mild variety. (OMG! That's it! I've been trying to come up with the perfect title for the one-man Broadway musical revue I'll undoubtedly win a Tony Award for one day. Just picture it on a marquee, spelled out in lightbulbs: "Ross Mathews in Chunky Mild Variety." Suck on that, *Hamilton*!)

Yep, I've turned down a lot of reality TV shows. But don't get me wrong—despite my reservations about appearing on them, I absolutely love watching them. I'll go out on a limb here and say reality TV is an even more important and revolutionary invention than the Squatty Potty. And honey, the Squatty Potty is the shit!

Yes, I love reality TV. Like a loaded baked potato, a full-body massage, or a full-body massage while eating a loaded baked potato, reality TV is the ultimate guilty pleasure.

With reality TV, there's no annoying concentrating or pesky thinking. Who needs complicated backstories or plotlines? Not this guy! Nope, all I need is drunk middle-aged women flipping over tables, hot-bodied and sexually questionable guys handing out roses to desperate single ladies, and former sitcom stars ballroom dancing in pants so tight, there's—ironically—no ball room.

Because I love reality TV shows so much, it may be hard to believe that I've never really wanted to be on one, but it's just the truth. Listen, I'm not delusional about my level of fame. I'd like to think I'm still trying to climb my way up the ladder of show business success, hoping to prove that my popularity, profile, and possibilities are growing, not shrinking. And let's be honest—a lot of reality TV is a junkyard for *former* stars, not *future* stars. It's for has-beens, not gonna-bes. It's for "OMG, he's still alive?" not "OMG, I live for him!"

So even though I've adored spending countless hours watching mindless and melodramatic models, morons, and man-candy, I always worried that doing one of those shows would be like flying too close to the sun. I mean, I love watching *Intervention*, *Hoarders*, and *Live PD*, but I've never had a desire to be on those shows, either. Make sense?

So the first time I was officially offered a gig on a reality TV show, I immediately said no. It was in 2005 and VH1 asked me to be on the fifth season of their popular show *Celebrity Fit Club*—a show that forced celebs to diet, compete in hard-core fitness challenges, and weigh in on national television. Let me repeat that last part: WEIGH IN ON NATIONAL TELEVISION.

Oh, hell, no. Homo don't play that!

So I followed my gut—my soft, flabby gut—and turned them down. Sure, I had weight to lose, but I certainly had no intention of doing it on air with the whole world watching, thank you very much, *so they could take their stupid TV show and shove it up their—*

And then they told me how much it paid.

"When do we start?"

Girl, I may have standards, but I'm also a whore who has a price tag. My artistic integrity went out the window faster than I could say, "I'd like two extra-large Meat Lover's Stuffed-Crust

Pizzas with ranch on the side, please" into the phone the night before I reported for shooting (ummm, hello—everyone knows you're legally entitled to a "death row meal" before you start any good diet).

The cast competing that season was a plethora of pop culture pudgies: rappers Warren G and Da Brat, eighties pop sensation Tiffany, *American Idol* contestant Kimberley Locke, comedy country crooner Cledus T. Judd, as well as iconic sitcom superstars Maureen "Marcia Marcia Marcia" McCormick from *The Brady Bunch* and Dustin "Screech" Diamond from *Saved by the Bell*.

And then there was me . . . Not a rapper, not a singer, not a sitcom star. Just a guy who interviewed celebrities on red carpets. A guy who not only needed the paycheck, but who needed to lose a li'l weight. You know, those last forty pounds of stubborn baby fat?

Going into the experience, I just assumed that it would be like what I had seen on NBC's *The Biggest Loser*, another reality competition show about fatties fighting their food fixations. I thought to myself, *I'm sure there'll be a team of experts offering a round-the-clock support and calorie-counting camaraderie. Certainly there will be dieticians-to-die-for and top-of-the-line trainers. And at the very least, there will be healthy craft services and a hot guy in short-shorts named Chip spotting me while I lift weights, his junk precariously close to my starving face, right? Right?!?*

Wrong. *Celebrity Fit Club* was the redheaded stepchild of weight-loss shows. Unlike the contestants on *The Biggest Loser*, we didn't live in a house together, we didn't have access to 24/7 support, and we were mostly left to our own devices. And, for the record, my own "devices" were an ice cream scooper and a pizza cutter, so . . . good luck, Shamu.

Every two weeks the entire cast would gather together to film an episode where we'd compete as teams in physically grueling challenges like obstacle courses in the woods, BMX biking, and ballroom dancing while licensed paramedics stood by with stretchers and oxygen tanks just in case.

And then, adding insult to obstacle course–related injury, they'd weigh us. One by one. In front of each other. On national television. It was humiliating.

Even though I led my team to victory, gained some friends, and lost some weight, I ultimately didn't love the experience. Call me crazy, but it was hard for me to care whether or not I could kayak faster than Da Brat or beat Screech at kickboxing. Ironically, I just couldn't stomach it.

So as soon as we finished filming, I did two things: vowed to never do another reality show again and ordered a take-home Italian pasta dinner for four: me, myself, and I . . . and myself again later that night.

And I managed to avoid doing another reality show for more than a decade. That is, until I was given an offer I simply couldn't refuse.

I have loved CBS's *Big Brother* since the first season debuted way back in 2000. I remember seeing commercials for it and being in awe. Good-looking people locked away in a house, completely closed off from the outside world, jockeying for power, manipulating their fellow houseguests, and—most importantly—showering on camera? That is literally everything I ever want to watch.

So since Season 1, episode one, I have been a staunch supporter and devoted viewer. In fact, if you rewatch the first season finale, you can see my head in the audience. I stole a piece of bark

from the front yard of the *Big Brother* house as a souvenir and, true story, I still have it.

Part of the fun of watching *Big Brother* is talking smack as the players mess up. I love to scream at my TV, "What is that dummy doing? Oh, please, that's not how you play the game! Why'd he nominate her for eviction? So stupid!"

Oh, yeah, I'd bragged many a time about knowing exactly how I'd play *Big Brother* and how I'd make it to the end. After watching literally hours of game play, my formula for success was simple: You needed to find one close ally you could trust, make multiple alliances so you could easily pivot to wherever the power lay in the house, and you had to win challenges whenever your ass was on the line.

It's easy to think you have all the answers when you're merely a *Big Brother* backseat driver or armchair quarterback, and I slept easy at night knowing I'd never have to actually prove my strategy was fail-safe. That is until I heard CBS was doing a celebrity version of the show. As a fan, I was thrilled. As a human being, I was terrified. Why? Because I just knew they were gonna ask me to be on the show. I called my manager, Mark. "I hope CBS doesn't offer me *Celebrity Big Brother*."

He was confused. "Why not? You'd be great. You've always said you'd know how to make it to the end."

"Exactly! But that was easy to say in my living room! I don't wanna actually *do* it, but I know if they ask I won't be able to say no!"

He reassured me, "Well, maybe they won't even ask you to do it."

"No," I was certain. "They're gonna call. I feel it."

And I was right. About a month later, Mark called me. "You

won't believe it. CBS just called. Wanna move into the *Big Brother* house?"

Fuck. No, I didn't want to do it. Put my life on hold, leave my house, and live with strangers on TV? No, I didn't want to do it. But I knew I had to. The superfan in me couldn't say no.

But I had some questions. So Mark set up a phone call with me and the producers. My first question? The most logical question I could think of. The question you'd probably ask first, too: "Is there a camera pointed at the toilet?"

"There usually is," they answered, "but for the celebrity version we've removed it. There is a microphone in there, though."

Microphones in the toilet? Suddenly I felt flushed. This was a horrible idea. I shouldn't do this.

"I'll do it."

Even now, I don't know why I ultimately said yes. At the time, my life was very complicated. My mother was battling breast cancer, another close family member was just entering rehab, and my relationship was going through a bit of a rough patch. I felt like I had nothing left to give. I needed to recharge, but how?

Everyone was leaning on me, and although I was happy to be there for people I loved, I have to admit I was emotionally exhausted. I remember one day, after my phone rang for what seemed like the four thousandth time, screaming, "I just wish I could go somewhere no one could contact me!"

So when I was offered *Celebrity Big Brother*, the idea of escaping reality to do a reality show for twenty-nine days seemed like just what I needed. Call it serendipity, call it kismet, call it fate. All I know is that the Universe heard my plea and knew what was best. So after getting my family's blessing to go away for so long and getting the producers to agree that they'd tell me if anything happened with my family's health while I was sequestered in the house, I signed the contract.

And I really was sequestered—no contact with the outside world, no internet, no phones. While inside the house, the only contact I had with humans other than my fellow houseguests was when I went into the Diary Room to talk to a producer. But, get this: I never actually saw anybody. Instead, I'd sit in a chair and talk to a camera as the producer's voice was piped in through a speaker. It was all so surreal.

I'll never forget the first time I walked into the *Big Brother* house. It was just like when Dorothy walked into Oz, except in place of the Tin Man there were cameramen, instead of a Cowardly Lion people would soon be cowardly lyin', and rather than a Wicked Witch, we had Omarosa.

Oh. My. Omarosa. She had just left the White House and was now walking into the *Big Brother* house to share a mic'd toilet with me and TEN other celebrities. Here's a sentence you never think you'll say: "Hey, Omarosa, can you hand me more toilet paper?"

Check. I've said it.

Very quickly, the other celebrities and I became fast friends. Here, in no particular order, is my take on each one of them:

- **Chuck Liddell:** I wasn't familiar with Chuck prior to *Big Brother*, mostly because I've never seen an MMA fight. I liked him right away, though. For somebody who made his living beating the shit out of other people, he was surprisingly easygoing and gentle. My favorite moment with Chuck was when he came upstairs for a spa day with me and the girls. We gave him an oatmeal facial and gossiped all afternoon. Of course, I knew it was game play on his part, but I didn't care. We had fun . . . and then we evicted him first. A threat is a threat!

- **Ariadna Gutiérrez:** Most famous for being mistakenly crowned Miss Universe by Steve Harvey, Ariadna is an angel on this earth. Every day Ari and I would cook together, and every night as we'd fall asleep, Ari would read her Bible to me in Spanish. I loved her, but knew I could never sit next to her in the final two because she'd win for sure.

- **Mark McGrath:** I had briefly worked with Mark at *Extra* a couple times back in the day and had seen him once at a Mexican restaurant in Toluca Lake (Don Cuco's—get the chicken fajitas!), but we weren't what you would call amigos. Inside the house, I trusted him right away and I would've taken him to the final two if I had won the last Head of Household competition.

- **Marissa Jaret Winokur:** Marissa was my savior in the house. Believe it or not, the Tony Award–winning actress and I didn't know each other before *Big Brother*, but we were instant besties. Nothing was going to come between us. If I hadn't had Marissa in the house, I don't think I would've enjoyed the experience nearly as much. After *Big Brother*, Marissa is one of my dearest friends.

- **James Maslow:** I wasn't aware of the band Big Time Rush, so I didn't know who their lead singer James was when I met him in the house, but I knew one thing right away: He had to go. He was too gorgeous, too charming, too athletic, and too hard to beat. Marissa and I cozied up to him, though, because we knew he would always be a bigger threat than us, and the other houseguests would keep him in their crosshairs rather than us.

- **Brandi Glanville:** I knew Brandi well before *Big Brother* (see the Brandi chapter in this book), and I was thrilled to see a familiar face in the house. That being said, I knew Brandi demanded loyalty, and *Big Brother* is a tough place to be loyal. Brandi made every day fun, though. From playing charades to playing with her extensions, we laughed constantly. Well, until I had to choose between her and Marissa and sent her home. She still hasn't forgiven me for that, but I promised to pay for happy hour for the rest of our lives, so we're doing fine.

- **Metta World Peace:** Basketball isn't my forte, but I'd still heard of Metta. I mean, hello, this is an all-star who won an NBA Championship with the LA Lakers. Plus his name is *Metta World Peace*. He's kind of hard to ignore. Metta and I clicked right away. We were like that movie *Twins* and Metta was the Danny DeVito.

- **Keshia Knight Pulliam:** Everyone knows Rudy Huxtable, and I wanted to scream for joy when she walked into the house. Keshia was super-nice, but she had just had a baby and was understandably struggling. The producers set up an area in the storage room where Keshia could pump her breast milk, and they'd send it off to her baby, who was staying at a hotel nearby with Keshia's mother. Eventually, it became too difficult for Keshia, and she asked that we send her home. Of course we did. I'd say she "milked" that opportunity, but that would be tacky.

- **Shannon Elizabeth:** I respected *American Pie* actress Shannon right away because I could tell she was smart, an animal activist, and clearly the best player in the game: athletic, aggressive, and cutthroat. Plus, I remembered that she was a competitive poker player, so I knew she was strategic. She won the first Head of Household competition, as well as the first Power of Veto. She was a threat and I knew she'd come after me the first chance she got. Eventually, we all rallied to evict her from the house, and she didn't take it well. I was honestly shocked—Shannon was the biggest fan of *Big Brother* in the house. Maybe even bigger than me. I thought she'd respect the game play, shake my hand, and say, "Good move." She didn't do that. In fact, she still has never spoken to me since *Big Brother*. I felt guilty until months later when Marissa sent me a YouTube clip of Shannon scheming in the house with Omarosa about getting the two of us out. Now I don't feel guilty anymore.

- **Omarosa:** You have to remember when this all went down. Mere weeks before entering the *Big Brother* house, Omarosa had been working as director of communications for the Office of Public Liaison in the Oval Office, alongside the most controversial president in the history of the United States of America. And when she walked into the

Big Brother house, I couldn't believe my eyes. Omarosa was reality TV royalty and I was scared shitless.

The moment she saw me, she said, "Oh, my gosh, Ross! You're the biggest threat in the house."

Immediately I thought to myself, *This bitch has got to go.* Even though I thought she was right (hello—I was the biggest threat!) and I respected her hustle, I knew Omarosa had tons of reality TV experience, was major competition, and had to be evicted ASAP. But I also wasn't stupid—I knew having her on the show meant huge ratings. Even though we were sequestered from the outside world and had no clue what was going on beyond our four walls, I knew the fact that Omarosa was in the house meant one thing: Millions of Americans were watching to see what she'd say about her former boss, our commander in chief.

I also knew that, in addition to trying to win *Celebrity Big Brother*, I also had to try to win Omarosa over. America needed me to get the scoop. So one night, as we were all sitting on the back patio, I waited patiently as each houseguest headed to bed. Eventually it was just me and the big O in the backyard. I knew this was my chance. The following is our conversation verbatim. You can watch it on YouTube.

I gently made my approach. "Omarosa, can we talk?"

She leaned forward. "Sure . . ."

I went in. "From the outside, can I tell you as a voter, a citizen, I never got it . . . why you went to the White House with him."

I could tell she wanted to talk. "I felt like it was like a call of duty," she whispered. "I was serving my country, not serving him."

I nodded. "That makes sense," I agreed, trying to make her feel comfortable while channeling my inner Anderson Cooper.

"It was always about the country." Then she really started opening up, explaining what it was like behind the scenes. "Like, I was haunted by tweets every single day, like, what was he gonna tweet next?"

I wanted to ask the questions I thought people really cared about. "Does anybody say to him, 'What are you doing?'"

She took a deep breath and explained, "I mean, I tried to be that person, and then all of the people around him attacked me. It was like 'Keep her away, don't give her access, don't let her talk to him . . .'"

And then something happened that I never thought I'd see, not in this lifetime. Omarosa began to . . . cry? Yes. Those were tears! The seemingly coldhearted woman who originated the role of Reality Show Villain was now crumbling in front of me. I simultaneously felt two things: one, like I wanted to give Omarosa a hug, and two, like the new motherfuckin' Barbara Walters!

As Omarosa wiped tears away, I continued to press, knowing America needed me. "Who has the power to say, 'What's going on?'"

Omarosa looked down and shook her head. "I don't know, I'm not there. It's not my circus, not my monkeys. I'd like to say 'Not my problem,' but I can't say that because . . ." She paused, knowing that the words coming out of her mouth were bombshells that would be dissected and analyzed by the entire nation. She uttered gravely, her voice trembling and nearly inaudible, ". . . It's bad."

I felt like I spoke for a lot of people when, rather than words coming out of my mouth, I just uttered a guttural "Ugh," and continued, "Don't say that . . ."

This was huge. I knew without a doubt that this would be breaking news around the world when it aired. I also knew that this kind of insight—a firsthand look at what was going on be-hind the scenes during the most tumultuous political time of my lifetime—was very rare and probably wouldn't happen again, so I wanted to ask the questions that would concern real people.

I remember thinking about people who work hard every day, but can still barely pay the bills. I thought about moms and dads who struggle to keep just their heads above water, let alone save for their kids' college. I thought about people like my parents who always wanted the best for me, even if it meant sacrificing things for themselves. I asked myself, *What did they want to know?*

Suddenly the simplest request I could think of seemed utterly profound. I pleaded with Omarosa, "We are worried, but I need you to say, 'No, it's gonna be okay.'"

Omarosa had been privy to the goings-on inside Trump's inner circle from the very beginning. If the media had in fact blown this all out of proportion and the very values of the Con-stitution and the country were not really at stake, she could put a lot of people at ease by just saying, "Yes."

But she didn't do that. She shook her head, held back tears, and said to me and an entire viewing nation, "No, it's not gonna be okay . . . It's not."

And with that I looked away, took a deep breath, and sighed. It was late and Omarosa and I were the only two houseguests still up. She said good night and gave me a hug. The truth is, I think Omarosa knew what she was doing. She had come into the *Big Brother* house for two reasons: She loved the game and she wanted to rehab her image. I think she did a fucking great job at both.

As soon as I saw her close her bedroom door, I burst into the Diary Room. It was about 2 a.m., but I knew there were always producers available. I had to make sure they'd seen that conversation. With one hundred cameras taping twenty-four hours a day, I was worried my groundbreaking future Pulitzer Prize–winning exclusive interview might go unnoticed. "Hello? Hello?"

It took the producer a minute to answer.

"Hey, Ross. Yeah. What's up?"

"Umm, I don't wanna tell anyone how to produce their show, but, umm . . . DID YOU JUST FUCKING SEE MY CONVERSATION WITH OMAROSA?!?"

There was a pause. Just silence. The producers have to be very careful how they talk to us, so as to make sure they don't have favorites, let outside information in, or give us any hints of how the show is being edited. As a producer myself, I respected that. But I needed them to cut through the bullshit now and talk to me, human to human. Thankfully, the producer bent the rules—just a little, just this once, just a bit.

Her voice came on the speaker, giggly and excited. She whispered, "Are you fucking kidding me? I was glued. It's 2 a.m., but I'm texting all the producers now. Holy shit, Ross."

I knew it! I leaned back in my chair and said, "When I'm on the news tomorrow, make sure they spell my name right: one 't' in Mathews. Good night!"

She laughed. "Good night, Ross."

The next morning, I went back into the Diary Room. "I'm on CNN right now, aren't I?"

"Ross," the producer said, "you know I can't tell you that."

I didn't need her to confirm it. I knew I was. And you know what? I found out after I left the house that I was. Not just on CNN, either: My convo with O was on Fox News and *Good Morning America* and the *Today* show and you name it, we were on it. Meghan McCain called me "the new Edward R. Murrow" on *The View*. Nicolle Wallace called me "amazing" on *Deadline: White House*. The White House even had to address my chat with Omarosa from the podium in the press room.

I've spent my entire life worshiping pop culture, and the one time I was actually part of it, I was sequestered inside a house sharing a shower with Metta World Peace. Well, ain't that a bitch.

I ended up coming in second place in *Celebrity Big Brother*, runner-up to my *CBB* BFF, the phenomenal Marissa Jaret Winokur. And yes, I totally agree with you—I should've won. But I was voted America's Favorite Houseguest by the fans, and at the end of the day, that honestly meant more to me than winning. I'd sat on my couch watching nearly twenty seasons of *Big Brother*, bragging about how I'd make it to the end if I ever got the chance to play. And you know what? I did. And the fact that the viewers saw what I did is more important to me than anything else.

After I left the house, I was overcome with emotion. I know it was just a silly reality show, but being sequestered from the outside world gave me a lot of time to think about myself, my life, and my choices. As much as I had enjoyed temporarily escaping from my complicated life, and spending some amazing time bonding with my *Big Brother* "family"—I had a real family I couldn't wait to get home to. A family that, I was thrilled to learn upon my exit, was doing great. My relative in rehab was showing up, doing the work, and healing. I had gained some important insight into my strained relationship. My mother was bravely fighting cancer—and winning! And last, but by no means least, my dogs Audrey and Selena were the same precious little stinkers they had been when I had tearfully said goodbye to them over a month earlier.

Oh, and once the cameras stopped rolling, Omarosa also told me some other shit that I'm too scared to put into this book. The day after we got out of the *Celebrity Big Brother* house, we all met up at Marissa's house to finally talk about all the stuff no one wanted to mention while cameras had been rolling twenty-four hours a day. Like a scene right out of a spy movie, Omarosa made us all put our phones in a corner, and then she spilled some serious White House tea that shook us all to the core. She dramatically swore us all to secrecy. I agreed, although in the back of my mind I thought I may share it in a book one day. You guys, it was way too juicy to keep to myself. Plus, I knew Omarosa pretty well by now, so she didn't scare me! That is until I walked her out of Marissa's house that afternoon and saw two security guards waiting to escort her into a black SUV.

I thought to myself, OMG, *WTF? Is that the FBI, the CIA, or maybe her SUV had just gotten a flat tire and they're fancy mechanics from AAA?*

Right after they whisked Omarosa away, I swear to God a scary black helicopter right out of a Tom Cruise summer blockbuster flew over. Was it her security? The government watching? Or just a news helicopter headed to cover a story? I'll never know for sure, but I wasn't about to mess with that shit. I'm no fool! I may have beat Omarosa at *Celebrity Big Brother*, but my ass can't compete with two security guards and a mysterious helicopter. You win, girl! You win.

CHAPTER ELEVEN

A Dollop of Divas

COCKTAIL

Diva Daiquiri

¼ cup rum

½ tablespoon fresh lime juice

1½ tablespoons simple syrup (girl, you should know how to
make it by now—I've told you like ten times)

Combine rum, lime juice, and simple syrup with ice. Shake and
serve with a garnish—berries, mint, whatever—express yourself
like a true diva!

A Date with a Diva

A dozen large Medjool dates

Goat cheese

Bacon

Slice dates in half and remove the pit. Stuff the dates with goat cheese and wrap each with half a slice of bacon, securing with a toothpick. Place bacon-wrapped dates on a baking sheet covered in either nonstick tinfoil or parchment paper. Bake at 400° until the bacon is well done (20–25 minutes). Allow them to cool before serving.

SOMETIMES, AFTER EVEN the fanciest dinner party, the thing you remember most is not the main course, but a particularly tasty appetizer. Was the prime rib good? Of course. But those bacon-wrapped, goat cheese–stuffed Medjool dates? Those were off the charts!

Well, these stories about my encounters with some very famous divas are just like that. Simply because these stories may not be long enough to warrant their very own chapter, their star power is simply too delicious to omit. What follows is a collection of tiny anecdotes, easily digestible side dishes that should be thought of as finger foods of fame, nutritious nuggets of name-dropping—very amusing amuse-bouches, if you will.

Bon appétit!

Liza Minnelli

COCKTAIL

Life Is a Cabernet, Ol' Chum

Simple glass of a hearty, deep, well-rounded Cabernet
Sauvignon

ROSSIPE

Baked Ziti with a Z

1 pound dry ziti pasta

1 pound ground turkey

Palmful crushed red pepper

1 large white onion, chopped

2 cloves garlic, chopped

1 packet taco seasoning

1 can diced tomatoes

1 can sliced black olives

1 can Ortega green chiles

1 cup sour cream

6 ounces mozzarella cheese

6 ounces sharp cheddar cheese

Fresh cilantro

Boil a large pot of salted water. Once it's boiling, add dry ziti
pasta and cook until al dente (8–10 minutes). Meanwhile, brown

the ground turkey with the crushed red pepper, chopped onion, and garlic (add the garlic last so it doesn't burn). Add the packet of taco seasoning, can of tomatoes, sliced black olives, and green chiles, simmer, and remove from heat. Mix in the cooked ziti pasta, sour cream, and half of each type of cheese (mozzarella and cheddar). Spread the entire mixture into a casserole dish and cover with the rest of the mozzarella and cheddar. Bake at 350° for 30–45 minutes, or until the cheese is melted and bubbling. Serve with chopped cilantro sprinkled over it.

The first time I ever saw Liza Minnelli was in the movie *Arthur* when I was around five years old, and boy, did she leave quite an impression on me. I remember thinking, even then, *What in the hell is wrong with this woman?!?*

She delivered every line so strangely, as if it were a punchline, even when it wasn't. Of course, as an adult, this kookiness is now something I absolutely adore about Liza. But as a kid, I just thought she was weird.

As I grew up, my fascination with Liza also grew, but it morphed from confusion into full-tilt obsession as I ravenously consumed every movie she ever made. *Cabaret, The Sterile Cuckoo, New York, New York,* just to name a few. I remember braving the cold Pacific Northwest weather and trekking to my local Blockbuster Video store in four feet of snow, both ways, to rent these films on VHS and hoping against hope that they weren't already checked out. (Looking back, what was I thinking? It's not like there was an army of other twelve-year-old, chubby, prepubescent Liza superfans I had to fight off.)

Yes, kids, back in the day, you had to go out into the world and track down the quality entertainment you craved. I couldn't just sit on my lazy ass and have YouTube do all the work for me, serving up a heaping helping of Liza classics, one after another. These days, I can pour myself a big glass of Chardonnay, fire up my laptop, and happily fall down a Minnelli rabbit hole for hours. Oh, and you haven't lived until you've seen me do my rendition of "Ring Them Bells" from *Liza with a Z* at karaoke. Showstopper! No, seriously . . . people always want the show to stop.

And then it happened . . . my first real-life Liza sighting. It was on the streets of New York. And wow—she was a vision to behold. She was crossing the street in the classic "look at me" disguise that so many celebrities wear: giant sunglasses. (Um, you know we can see you, right?)

Obviously the disguise worked, though, because she was managing to weave her way along the busy New York sidewalk completely unnoticed. But not by me, honey! Oh, please. I knew it was Liza the moment I saw her signature shock of spiky jet-black hair. And what was she wearing, you ask? Oh, just the simplest Ed Hardy sweat suit—BeDazzled from head to toe, of course. She looked perfect.

When I saw her, I froze, right there in the middle of the sidewalk. I couldn't move. I couldn't think. I couldn't breathe. My body went into Gay Icon Survival Mode.

Randomly seeing Liza crossing the street is like spotting Bigfoot while camping. What is one to do? Well, there are two options: either run away or silently follow the creature from a safe distance and observe it in its natural habitat. Guess which option I chose. Um, duh.

I sneakily followed Liza into a restaurant. Why? BECAUSE

THAT IS JUST WHAT MY BODY INSTINCTIVELY DID. Please don't judge me.

It didn't matter what plans I had scheduled that afternoon—a doctor's appointment, a previous commitment to volunteer at an orphanage, an exclusive, one-on-one interview with President Barack Obama—all that obviously went right out the window as I stealthily sat down just a few tables away from Liza and the friend she was lunching with. I felt like a private dick on a Liza kick.

I wasn't even hungry. I had already eaten before the Liza spotting, but I tried to blend in by ordering myself a bowl of soup. Or *shoup*, as Liza would say. The adorable way she pronounces her Ss—like she's gargling glitter—is one of the things I love most about her. Things aren't just super, they're *shuper!* Liza doesn't wear sequins, she wears *shequins!* And it's really hard to stay depressed when you're feeling *shad* instead of sad.

Sho I sat there *shlurping* my *shoup*, watching as Liza did the best Liza impersonation I had ever seen—and I've seen a lot! If I had a dollar for every drag queen to whom I've given a dollar as they lip-synched one of her signature songs, I'd be swimmin' in coin like Scrooge McDuck from *DuckTales*. (Not to digress, but does anyone else find it really disturbing when he dives into that money vault filled to the brim with coins? I mean, that's gotta hurt! I'd hate to see the medical bill for that duck bill!)

Liza was exactly as I'd imagined, like a Muppet on meth, her arms gesticulating and her head bouncing around like a rubber ball with a Liza wig on it. It's almost as if she knew I was watching and thought, *Okay, let's give this queen the whole Liza experience!*

I didn't approach her. I don't know why, exactly. I asked myself, *Why aren't you saying hi?* Maybe I was scared? I didn't even try to make eye contact. I just watched from afar, just grateful to be that near her. Also, I think I knew deep down that one day—someday—I would meet her for real, and without having to innocently stalk her in a restaurant.

And I was right! That day came a few years later when I had the honor of sitting down to interview Ms. Minnelli to promote her Tony-nominated one-woman-show *Liza's at the Palace*. No sunglasses, no soup, no stalking. This time, she would actually know that I was in the room with her. Was I excited? Uhhh, is the first song in her iconic televised musical special *Liza with a Z* titled "Yes"?!? (Yes, it is.)

The setup for the interview was simple: two director's chairs in front of a black curtain. I remember taking my seat, waiting for Liza to arrive, and feeling like I was about to meet with royalty . . . because I *was*. This icon of film, stage, and Studio 54 was fifty-four seconds from sitting across from me, and I was just trying to breathe. Then, suddenly, she burst in, sat down, and exclaimed, "Hi there, shweetie!"

Liza was a delight—so fun, so energetic, so present. The whole conversation was a whirlwind. Before I knew it, the interview was almost over, and without thinking, I asked Liza a question I immediately regretted.

"Could you show me how to do jazz hands?"

The moment it came out of my mouth, I wished I could take it back. I mean, this wasn't some sitcom star or reality TV flash in the pan. This was Liza Freakin' Minnelli. This was Judy Garland's daughter! This was an EGOT-winning legend, an iconic *shupershtar* who had an Emmy, two Grammys, an Oscar, and *four* Tonys on her mantel! The only Oscar I will ever have is a vintage stuffed Oscar the Grouch doll. I may have four Tonys, but they're all Italian friends of mine. You know what's on my mantel? A participation ribbon from a pie-eating contest and a dead succulent. Do you know how hard it is to kill a freakin' succulent?!

Time stopped as Liza just stared at me. *Great,* I thought. *I've blown it.* And then, without a word, Liza suddenly leapt out of her seat, planted her feet, and shot her right arm into the air, wiggling her fingers like a posse of possessed snakes. "LIKE THISH!" she shouted, laughing hysterically.

God, I love her.

Then she hugged me and, still laughing, pulled me close to her and said, in her signature Liza voice, "Sherioushly, congratulationsh on all your shucshesh!"

Liza with an OMG.

Christina Aguilera

Dirrty Xtini

6 ounces vodka

1 dash dry vermouth

1 ounce olive juice (from jar)

4 green olives

Combine vodka, vermouth, and olive juice in a shaker with ice. Shake and strain into a martini glass. Add olives. This drink is beautiful, no matter what they say.

ROSSIPE

Ain't No Other Ham Rollup

Pimento cheese

Slices of deli ham

1 can fried onions crisps

Spread pimiento cheese onto a slice of deli ham and sprinkle fried onion crisps on top. Roll up and slice into sushi-shaped pieces. So tacky, but sooooo delicious!

Remember that time I went "on tour" with Christina Aguilera? No? Well, it was only one city for a *Tonight Show* segment, so if you blinked you probably missed it.

The whole idea of the piece was that she saw me become BFFs with Gwyneth Paltrow and go to London with her on air, and now she wanted to be my BFF. Yeah, that's right, I had two of the hottest blond celebrity babes fighting for my attention. *Ladies, ladies . . . there's enough of me to go around!*

At a certain point in the early 2000s, every red-blooded American boy had to make a choice: Was he a Britney or an Xtina? Let me tell you, for a gay boy, this was more painful than Sophie's Choice. But, ultimately, it turned out—after much thought, deliberation, and prayer—that I was an Xtina. I mean, that voice! Oh, and the fact that she didn't use filthy public gas station restrooms while barefoot helped, too. Sorry, but that's a deal breaker, Brit-Brit!

My *Tonight Show* crew and I traveled to Dallas, Texas, where Christina was on tour with the man who will forever be known for tearing apart the best boy band since the Beatles, Justin Timberlake (*NSYNC 4-EVA!). Yes, Justin was bringing Sexy Back and I was bringing Sexy Back Fat. This was before I discovered Man Spanx, so cut me some back slack.

When Xtina and I met for the first time, it was Xtra Xciting! We met on-camera hugging and gushing and giggling, just like real-life friends. She was so sweet. I was kind of nervous she'd be different when the cameras were off. But you know what? She wasn't. In fact, she was even sweeter and more vulnerable.

We shot a ton of backstage footage: in her dressing room, playing with her costumes, learning moves with her amazing backup dancers. Then I got to sit front row at her show, in a crowd of more than twenty thousand fans packed into Dallas's American Airlines Center.

When she ended her show, singing an encore of "Beautiful," she walked to the edge of the stage, held my hand, and sang it directly to me. This really happened! And I can prove it, because the *Tonight Show* cameras captured it all. To this day, if I ever feel less-than-glamorous or if I have a blemish or if I'm having a bad hair day, I just remember Christina Aguilera staring into my eyes and telling me that I am beautiful. I am still waiting to hear it from Justin Timberlake, but that's another story.

After the concert, once we had wrapped our *Tonight Show* shoot and as she was getting into a van, she said, "We're going to a club tonight if you want to come."

I blurted out "YES!" so fast that my lips suffered minor whiplash.

When we got to the club, security herded us into a VIP area, corralled into a corner booth behind a velvet rope, like the world's most glamorous livestock. At one point, a fan sent her a drink. *How nice,* I thought. She said, "Thank you," took the drink, and then put it on a table away from her. "Never drink anything someone sends you. Unless you see the bartender make it, don't drink it."

Then she told me a fascinating story about how tough it is in the music industry and how hard she had to fight to be successful. I was riveted, hanging on her every word. Then she wrapped up her story with "And that's why I wrote 'Fighter.'"

Now whenever I tell a story about how tough something is—a recent trip to the DMV, happy hour trivia, my steak at Sizzler—I always end it with, "And that's why I wrote 'Fighter.'"

As the club was closing, she said, "Wanna come back to my hotel?"

I should be in the *Guinness Book of World Records* as the person who screamed "YES!" faster than any other person in human history.

Now, I have seen a lot of hotel suites, but this was hotel *sweet!* We were all just hanging out—Christina, me, and maybe fifteen or twenty other people. But, just like when you fall madly in love, as far as I was concerned there was no one in the room but me and my new straight-girl best friend, who just happened to be world-famous pop superstar Christina Aguilera. The relationship between a gay man and a straight woman is a sacred one. Throughout history, powerful women have always had their sassy gay sidekick. You just know that Cleopatra and her bitchy hairdresser would spend hours gossiping about men, fashion, and the latest trends in eyeliner as he meticulously braided her gorgeous hair. Think about it . . . Joan Crawford had Billy Haines, Sarah Jessica Parker has Andy Cohen, and Liza has, well, just about every man she has ever dated.

So we were all in the kitchen talking and laughing while Christina sat on the counter, "holding court" as they say. Before I knew it, it was around 4 a.m. and I heard Christina's beefy security guard telling everyone that it was time to go. Not one to ever overstay my welcome—okay, except maybe at a Red Lobster during Crabfest—I took my cue and started to leave. "Good night, thanks for everything."

Christina whispered, "Where are you going?"

I said, "You must be exhausted and security is kicking everyone out."

She said, "Only the people I don't know. Not you."

Listen, I have watched enough Oprah to know that self-confidence, happiness, and satisfaction are supposed to come from *inside* you. But at that moment I felt a rush of surface-level, ego-driven, ultra-shallow happiness one rarely feels. It's like when the hottest guy in the room flirts with you, or you hit the jackpot on the penny slots, or Christina Aguilera kicks everyone out of her ginormous hotel suite except for you. This magical feeling is rare, so when it comes along, just enjoy it!

So, to make a long story short—*too late!*—Christina and I talked about life and love and everything until the sun came up at 7 a.m.

I was so tired. Ask anyone who knows me, I am usually in bed with my dogs by 10 p.m. Years of waking up super-early have made me one of those annoying morning people. But this magical night with Christina was worth it all.

And that's why I wrote "Fighter."

Jackie Collins

COCKTAIL

Jackie Tom Collins

2 ounces gin

2 ounces club soda

½ ounce simple syrup

Juice of half a lemon

Combine all ingredients in a shaker with ice, shake, and strain into a glass with ice cubes. Drink with friends and tell a filthy joke in Jackie's honor.

ROSSIPE

Best Celery Bites

¼ cup balsamic vinegar

½ cup pine nuts

1 head of celery

1 package goat cheese

½ cup pomegranate seeds

Heat balsamic vinegar in a saucepan on medium heat, stirring often, until it thickens slightly. Heat pine nuts in a pan on low until they're slightly toasted. Meanwhile, cut celery into 1-inch-long pieces. Fill them with goat cheese, sprinkle with pomegranate seeds and toasted pine nuts, then drizzle with balsamic reduction. These Best Celery Bites are fit for a Best Seller!

Legendary author and socialite Jackie Collins and I met on Twitter. It was during the height of *Chelsea Lately*, which was also back when Twitter was still fun and new. I loved going directly home right after we taped the show to live-tweet when the show aired a couple hours later, reading every single comment and writing back to the viewers.

During one episode, as I was scrolling through my @'s, I noticed that one of the tweeters had one of those blue checkmarks next to their name. That, of course, meant the person commenting was famous and fabulous. But just how famous and fabulous I had no idea until I looked closer and saw that it was the one and only best-selling author and leopard print–loving sister of *Dynasty* star Joan Collins . . . JACKIE COLLINS!

Even her name sounded like one of her fictional characters who does scandalous things while wearing designer fashions featuring triple shoulder pads and an asymmetrical neckline. Ooh la la!

Yes, the Collins sisters were both stunningly beautiful, raven-haired man-eaters. How is it possible that one family could be blessed with so much glamour? I guess lightning struck twice. And Jackie wasn't just gorgeous, she was smart. And she had great taste in everything from chunky jewelry to chunky guys serving up comedy gold on TV talk shows. Yes, back to that tweet that had caught my eye . . .

For the life of me I cannot find the original, but I know it was something very sweet and complimentary, like "Watching *Chelsea Lately* and that Ross is so funny!"

My mind was blown. *Jackie Collins thinks I'm funny?!?* This woman had written dozens of best sellers and sold more than five hundred million copies, while simultaneously becoming a staple of the Beverly Hills social scene.

I quickly slid into Ms. Collins's DM's, thanking her for her comment, and—to my delight—she instantly replied!

Okay, let's play a game. What do you think Jackie Collins wrote to me after I thanked her?

1. "Awkward! I was only joking, honey. I find you and your insipid sense of 'humor' predictable and pedestrian. Blocking you immediately."

2. "Great! Is there any chance I can talk you into popping out of a giant cake at my sister Joan's birthday party this Thursday, wearing nothing but a hot-pink Speedo? Let me know ASAP."

3. "Darling, you're FAB! We must do dinner!"

If you guessed A, you're not only wrong, you're cruel. If you guessed B, you're not only wrong, you're a pervert. But if you answered C—*ding ding ding!*

Dinner? With a legend? Yes, please! I quickly accepted her generous invitation and began planning my outfit for my online date with a literary diva.

I left the restaurant up to Jackie, and of course she chose the best of the best—Beverly Hills hot spot Mr. Chow's. Fancy! I have to admit, I was a little nervous as I drove up to the valet, but I shouldn't have been. Ms. Collins and I hit if off immediately. Let's be honest, our life experiences couldn't have been more different. I mean, Jackie Collins was the picture-perfect poster child of opulence, the grande dame of glamour. And who was I? A former *Celebrity Fit Club* runner-up who made jokes on basic cable about people like Jessica Simpson for a living.

But it turns out there's a universal language that binds those from every background. And what is that language? The language of . . . gossip! Yes, honey! When in doubt, gossip it out!

Jackie soaked up pop culture and she simply lived to gossip. Fabulous celebrities? Yummy food? Juicy gossip? Needless to say, at dinner with Jackie, I was in Homo Hollywood Heaven!

Our marathon all-you-can-dish gossip dinners quickly became a tradition, continuing at all the A-list restaurants featuring the "in-crowd." Going to dinner with Jackie was like going to dinner with no one else. Jackie always got the very best table in the house, and at each restaurant, every famous person who entered the room would come up to her table to say hello. It was like a receiving line for the queen! The sweetest part? After saying hello, Jackie always included me, introducing me to all the stars. "Larry King, say hello to Ross Mathews. He's fabulous."

I felt just like Julia Roberts in *Pretty Woman*. You know, except for the high-end prostitute part.

I honestly have no idea where she found the time to write all those best-selling books of hers. First of all, she was always out to dinner! And secondly, she had five DVRs in her house! She recorded and watched *everything*. But somehow she still cranked out all those deliciously guilty pleasures like *Hollywood Wives* and *Lucky*—all written, she told me, in longhand on those yellow legal pads.

Jackie and I became great friends. Every year when she had a new book come out, she would send an autographed copy to both me and my mom. You've gotta love that.

I'll never forget that when I wrote my first best-selling book, *Man Up!*, Jackie came to the big launch party, and I overheard her telling a reporter something along the lines of "Twenty-two dollars for a book that's only 220 pages? What a ripoff! Mine are over 500 pages and the same price!"

What a bitch—I loved it! Let me tell you, if we had been characters in her sister Joan's campy prime-time soap opera from the 1980s, *Dynasty*, I probably would have wrestled with her in a shallow koi pond. But we weren't, so I didn't. Besides, I loved her. Jackie just always said what was on her mischievous mind. That was what made her so magical.

For instance, she invited me to a dinner party at her house once, and I had somehow put it in my schedule under the wrong date. When the day of the party arrived, she emailed me, "See you tonight!" I panicked, explaining that I had made a mistake, was actually away at my house in Palm Springs, and sadly, wouldn't able to attend.

"You just fucked up my entire seating arrangement!!!" she emailed back. "But I forgive you. You were seated between Raquel Welch and Kathy Griffin!" she added, knowing that missing out on being the meat in that sandwich was really twisting the knife. "Have fun in Palm Springs!"

The shade! I lived for it.

The next time she invited me to her house, you'd better believe I got the date right. When I first walked into her palatial Beverly Hills mansion, I gasped aloud. She just smiled and gave me the grand tour, knowing that many more gasps would escape

from my dropping jaw as she showed me amazing room after amazing room and fancy feature after fancy feature. She even had her very own art gallery, filled with breathtaking, and I assume expensive, paintings. And just when I didn't think I could gasp any more, she casually walked me over to the big picture window in the living room and pointed toward an equally impressive residence next door. "Oh, I own that house, too. Al rents it from me," she nonchalantly said, pausing for effect before she delivered the fatal blow, ". . . Pacino?"

I just laughed. "You just love saying that, don't you?"

She turned and walked away, slyly smiling. "Whatever do you mean, darling . . . ?"

After a few glasses of champagne, I had to pee. I asked Jackie which of the several powder rooms I had just seen on the house tour was for guests. "Use the one near the front door," she said, gracefully motioning toward the foyer.

When I walked in, I quickly realized I was in yet another "gallery" of sorts. The spacious powder room featured floor-to-ceiling framed photos of a smiling Jackie with every celebrity you could imagine: Michael Caine, Oprah, Sidney Poitier, Shirley MacLaine, John Travolta, and just about every other major star from the past thirty-five years or so.

I was so enthralled by the photos that I quickly forgot where I was and why I had gone in there. I must have spent at least fifteen minutes in the bathroom, staring at each and every photo. Looking at details like the jewelry that sitcom star from the seventies was wearing or the telltale facelift scars on that still handsome but very alert-looking leading man. Suddenly it dawned on me how long I'd been inside her bathroom! *Oh, my God!* I thought. *Jackie Collins must think I'm taking the biggest dump!*

I hurriedly did my business—just number one, I swear!—washed my hands, and ran out of the bathroom, screaming, "Jackie, I swear to God I just went pee!"

I explained that I had been looking at all the photos and I asked her if she thought maybe I would be hung in her bathroom one day. She thought it was hilarious.

I begged, "I want to be hung in your bathroom!"

She smiled, raised one perfectly tweezed eyebrow, and said, "Yes, and don't worry . . . you'll be very well hung, darling!"

Once, when I was guest-hosting *Chelsea Lately*, the producers asked me who I would like to have on as my guest. I knew Jackie was a fan of the show—after all, that's how we had met—and she had a new book coming out, so I said, "How about Jackie Collins? She's hilarious!"

The producers jumped at the chance. And Jackie was great. So charming and glamorous, but also very real. When I told the bathroom story on air, Jackie surprised me with a framed photo of us together. I reached out to take it, and she pulled it away from me and shook her head. "No," she said. "This one goes in the bathroom."

About a year or so later, I was in the car listening to the radio when the announcer said, "Best-selling author Jackie Collins died today of breast cancer at the age of seventy-seven . . ."

No one even knew she was sick. And as the shocking reality settled in, I flashed back to the last time I saw her. She was a guest on my podcast, *Straight Talk*. When she arrived at our studio in Beverly Hills, she had looked like her normal, gorgeous, put-together self. We had a terrific conversation on the show, covering ground we had never discussed before—all about her childhood and her family and her journey to becoming a literary legend. During that interview, I realized that, through the fancy dinners and endless gossip, we had formed a real, genuine, caring friendship.

I also remember telling her that day that she was the most fabulous person I had ever met, because, well, she was. And she still is. If you've never read one of her books, do yourself a favor and go pick one up. They're about five hundred pages, but only $22.

Faye Dunaway

COCKTAIL

Bonnie and Colada

3 cups frozen pineapple

1 soft banana

3 ounces white rum

⅔ cup coconut milk

Combine all ingredients in a blender and blend until smooth. Add more coconut milk if it's too thick. Garnish with a pineapple wedge.

Edamame Dearest

1 bag frozen edamame

1 lime

Tajin seasoning (available in most stores—a blend of salt, chili
powder, and lime)

Boil edamame for about 8 minutes and then drain them. Put in a
bowl, squeeze one whole lime over, and season generously with
Tajin seasoning. Using your teeth, squeeze the "beans" out and
enjoy. Trust me. SO good.

I don't know about you, but I like my movie stars a little cray cray.
And Faye Dunaway, let's be honest, leans a li'l loopy. And that's
not a diss! She's also a whole lotta talented, and I like that combination! Faye Dunaway is the kettle corn of Hollywood—sweet
and salty! And if your recipe includes one cup of kookoo and a
ton of talent, give me a big ol' bag of what you're poppin'!

So, just in case you've been living under a rock—or the only
thing you watch online is funny cat videos or drag queen makeup
tutorials—let me educate you on one of my favorite whack-
tresses, Faye Dunaway.

Ms. Dunaway has been in countless critically acclaimed
classic Hollywood films, like *Bonnie and Clyde*, *Chinatown*, and
Network. But, again, let's be honest—she is probably best known
for her infamous, scenery-chewing, all-but-career-ending por-
trayal of Joan Crawford in the mother of all camp classics,
Mommie Dearest. If you have not seen *Mommie Dearest*, stop

reading this book and go watch it right now. I'm serious. I can wait.

Welcome back. Amazing, right? Say what you will about *Citizen Kane* and *Gone with the Wind*, but I bet more people quote *Mommie Dearest* than those two "classy" movies combined.

I can't even imagine how people—especially gay people—expressed themselves before *Mommie Dearest* came out in 1981. Sometimes screaming "No wire hangers . . . EVER!" is the only proper response to someone who is annoying you. "I'm not one of your FANS!" is a timeless, foolproof way to make sure a friend doesn't let fame go to their head.

And I can't even begin to think how many times I have livened up a boring business meeting with an out-of-nowhere, well-timed "Don't fuck with me, fellas!"

Well, all these iconic lines of dialogue came flooding into my brain the night I saw the one and only Faye Dunaway imperiously walking down the press line at the *Vanity Fair* Oscar Party. I was on the line interviewing celebrities for *The Tonight Show* when I caught her out of the corner of my eye, briskly walking inside the party. I thought to myself, *Dear God, please don't let Dunaway get away!*

I yelled her name, "Ms. Dunaway! Ms. Dunaway!"

And to my surprise, she turned around and walked toward me. I immediately felt the undeniable star power emanating from her every pore. She was very beautiful, and my heart started pounding in my chest as I scrambled to think of something witty to say or ask. I had seen and heard more than one unlucky, misguided entertainment reporter step into the painful, rusty bear trap of bringing up *Mommie Dearest*—a film Faye obviously detested and avoided discussing despite the public's undying interest. It was almost as if she had completely cut the film from her credits and her memory—not unlike the scene where her character Joan Crawford cuts her ex-lover from dozens of framed photos: "If she doesn't like you, she can make you disappear!"

Not wanting to be bonked on the head with a can of powdered cleanser (you'll get it if you've watched the movie!), I decided to completely avoid *Mommie Dearest* and get on Faye's good side by bringing up one of her most popular and critically acclaimed films. A role for which she won the Oscar as Best Actress.

"*Network* is one of my favorite movies!" I said, thrusting my mic into her famous face. Something flashed in her iconic, almond-shaped eyes. For a brief moment I had no idea how she would respond. Or, for that matter, *who* would respond. Which of her many roles was crouching in her psyche just waiting to pounce on me? Would bank robber Bonnie Parker shoot me dead? Would psychic fashion photographer Laura Mars be able to read my mind and hear all those lines from *Mommie Dearest* echoing in there? Would I be ripped a new one by Joan Crawford herself?

But Faye just smiled at me, licked her lips, and said, "Good flick, good flick!"

Then she glided away as if on an invisible treadmill.

Huh? That's it? "Good flick"!? Wow. Looking back, I really should have just gone all *Mommie Dearest* on her ass. She probably would've hauled off and slapped me across the face. And that would have been such a better ending to this story than just "Good flick," am I right?

But I'm not hung up on it. After all, "NO WIRE HANGERS!!!"

Betty White

Betty White Russian

2 ounces vodka

1 ounce Kahlúa

½ ounce milk, heavy cream, or, if you're feeling festive,
eggnog!

Mix all ingredients, add ice, and enjoy out on the lanai with your three elderly roommates.

ROSSIPE

Cheesecake Bites

CRUST

1¼ cups crumbled graham crackers

1 tablespoon granulated sugar

⅓ cup unsalted melted butter

CHEESECAKE FILLING

16-ounce brick very soft, room-temperature cream cheese

¾ cup powdered sugar

1 teaspoon vanilla extract

Juice of ½ a lemon

1½ cups Cool Whip

Line a square or rectangle baking dish with parchment paper. In a bowl, combine the ingredients for the crust and mix. Then press into the bottom of the baking dish (I use a measuring cup and press down—it helps get the corners).

In a separate bowl, mix the cream cheese, powdered sugar, vanilla extract, and lemon juice. Then gently fold in Cool Whip. Spread over the crust and cool in refrigerator for 3–4 hours. Garnish with fresh berries and make sure to gather your best friends around the kitchen table.

Every human on this planet with a heartbeat knows which *Golden Girl* they are. The sluts are Blanche, the judgmental intellectuals are Dorothy, the sassy ones are Sophia, and the sweet ones are Rose.

I just adore them all, and I've even had the chance to work with one of them!

After *The Tonight Show with Jay Leno* became *The Tonight Show with Conan O'Brien*, it became *The Tonight Show with Jay Leno* again. For our first show back, we filmed a segment where Jay woke up from a dream, an obvious twist on the famous ending of *The Wizard of Oz*. He opened his eyes and looked around the room, surrounded by his bandleader Kevin Eubanks, me, and . . . Betty White! Jay said, "You were there, and you were there, and you were there . . ."

It was a funny bit, but what happened backstage made me laugh even more.

Betty was a pro. She knew all her lines and was the funniest person in the room. My friend Scott had booked her. Scott knew *everyone* and booked all the comics and celebrities for the many *Tonight Show* sketches. I've been friends with him since way before I was on the air. I used to deliver his mail, stopping to hang out and gossip with him before I had to continue with my mail delivery. Our gossip sessions were something we still enjoyed doing, but now with no pesky mail to get in the way. Scott was hilarious and sharp as a tack.

But that day Scott seemed . . . kind of *off*. He was confused and slurring his words. I was concerned. I pulled our stage manager over. "I'm worried about Scott. Come with me."

Scott lethargically mumbled, "Uh-oh, I did it again . . ."

What did he do? I thought. *Did he accidentally drink a keg of beer instead of coffee that morning? Did he scarf down three pot brownies for breakfast? Did he put black tar heroin in his breakfast burrito instead of turkey sausage?!*

He explained, "I must've taken an Ambien instead of my blood pressure pills this morning. Those damn bottles look exactly the same."

What a mess! The crew and I went into action. We tried to conceal Scott from everyone and sneak him out so he could go sleep it off in an office before anyone else noticed, but just then Jay and Betty walked up and started talking to us. I struggled to prop up Scott's limp, rubbery body. It was all very *Weekend at Bernie's.* (For the kids reading this, that's a movie about a dead guy, not a documentary about Labor Day with Bernie Sanders.) Then the sound guy, Kenny, came up to us. "Ms. White, would it be okay if I mic'd you up now?"

"Sure!" she said, lifting her arms up into the air so Kenny could easily attach her body mic and conceal the cord. When she lifted her arms, you could see just a little bit of Betty's midriff.

Scott, loopy as hell, pointed—like an uninhibited four-year-old—and loudly yelled, "BELLY WHITE!"

I have never laughed so hard in my life. But Betty didn't even bat an eyelash. After all, the woman had worked with the infamously hard-as-nails Bea Arthur for nearly a decade on *The Golden Girls*. I'm pretty sure she had heard much worse!

I quickly took Scott away and made sure he lay down to rest. As he was snoring, I tiptoed out of the room and tried to shut the door quietly. "Ross?" Scott called out.

"Yeah?"

"Thank you for being a friend."

Anne Bancroft

COCKTAIL

Agnes of Grog

2 ounces dark rum

½ ounce fresh lime juice

1 teaspoon brown sugar

4 ounces hot water

1 orange slice

1 cinnamon stick

What in the hell is grog, anyway? Well, you're in luck—I Googled it! In the eighteenth century, there was a British admiral named Edward Vernon, but everyone called him Old Grog for some silly reason. Anyway, the rumor is that he gave his soldiers a pint of rum every day to prevent scurvy. Not a very sexy story, but I thought not many of you would know what grog was. I certainly didn't. But I had to come up with a cocktail for Anne Bancroft, and since she was in the movie *Agnes of God*, this was the best I could do. Who knows? Maybe grog will become the next hot drink, and Lisa Vanderpump with start selling it for $25 a glass at Pump!

ROSSIPE

Mrs. RobinSun-Dried Tomato and Goat Cheese Puff Pastry Bites

1 package puff pastry

1 jar sun-dried tomato pesto

4 Roma tomatoes, sliced

1 package goat cheese

Salt and pepper, to taste

Fresh basil

This is so easy, but seems so fancy. Get a roll of puff pastry from the refrigerator section of your grocery store. Unroll, cut into 1½-inch squares, and place on a baking sheet lined with parchment paper. Spoon just a dab of sun-dried tomato pesto on each one. On top of that, place a slice of tomato. Finally, slice the goat cheese into ½-inch-thick pieces and put on top (make sure the goat cheese is cold—it's much easier to slice that way). Sprinkle with salt and pepper and bake 10–15 minutes at 375° or until the pastry looks golden brown. Sprinkle with chopped fresh basil.

New Year's Eve has always held a special place in my heart. It's the holiday of new beginnings and fresh starts. It's always a time to pause, reflect on what you've experienced, and focus on your upcoming goals. You know—goals like losing those extra five or ten or fifty pounds. Most years, I'm more festive than your aunt Helen after she drank the entire bottle of tequila you brought back from Mexico ("That was for everyone to share, Helen! And, please, put your blouse back on!"), but, for me, one year in particular wasn't so easy. In fact, it was hard as hell.

It was New Year's Eve 2003, and I was in New York City on assignment for a special live episode of *The Tonight Show*. As the famous ball dropped in Times Square that year, I was going to be doing the countdown, live on NBC. I hadn't been this excited about balls dropping since my own . . . even though my voice never really changed as promised. *Yoo-hoo, puberty! I'm still over here waiting!*

I was so excited to be in the epicenter of New Year's Eve, surrounded by tens of thousands of people celebrating and by millions of others watching from home. I could feel the electricity in the air. This was going to be one for the memory books. I could just feel it and I couldn't wait!

Just before I went live on the air my cell phone rang. It was my mom. "Happy New Year!" I happily yelled, simultaneously making her a part of the upcoming celebration *and* rehearsing my most important line of dialogue of the night. But my exhilaration quickly faded once I realized she was calling with bad news. Very bad news. My father, who had been bravely fighting cancer, was dying. "The doctors say he's only got two weeks."

Nothing ever prepares you for something like this. Everything else seemed meaningless. I looked around at thousands of people cheering and waving streamers in the air and I grew angry at them. *How can they celebrate when the world will never be the same? How am I gonna do this?* Logically I knew they had no idea what I was going through personally, but it still bothered me. It quickly became apparent that if I wanted to get through the night without screaming "Fuck all of you selfish drunk assholes, my dad is dying!" on live TV, I would have to at least muster up the strength to fake it. Yes, fake it. And that meant plastering a smile on my face and pretending like nothing was wrong.

I knew I had a job to do. I knew that millions of people would be tuning in to see confetti and lights and a big smile on my face. And I knew that if my dad were there to offer me advice, he would put his arm around me and say, "You can do it, son."

My dad wasn't just my biggest cheerleader; he was the man who had taught me how to be funny. And more important, he taught me how to use humor to cope with whatever life brought our way, no matter how painful.

And so I did it. It wasn't easy. There is a well-known phrase "Fake it till you make it," and I learned that night things don't become well-known phrases unless they're true. Okay, except maybe "One size fits all," but I digress. My point is that before I knew it, my smile felt less fake and I resented the rambunctious revelers a little less. After all, they were just celebrating life, right?

The next thing I knew I had let go and allowed myself to be embraced by the positive energy of all those people and focus on the tangible spirit of hope we were all collectively feeling that night. There are times when being in an enormous, overwhelming crowd such as that can seem like the loneliest place on Earth. And for a little while I definitely felt that. But later that night, the sensation eventually changed, and I actually felt "at one" with this throbbing, out-of-control throng of joyous party animals.

The next day, while most people slept until noon and nursed horrible hangovers, I was up bright and early to fly back home to Los Angeles. The party was over and the reality of the situation was as merciless as the morning sun in my bleary eyes. All I could think about was my dad, and I felt helpless. A flood of memories washed over me: all his love, all his support, all his dirty jokes.

As I found my seat on the plane, I saw a striking older woman walking down the aisle. She was very chic, with a fitted blazer and smart bob. She somehow seemed simultaneously strong, yet frail. Our eyes met and we smiled at one another. Just when I thought she was going to pass right by me, she stopped, grabbed my arm, and said, "Young man, I was home last night and not feeling very well. But I watched you on TV and you made me laugh. That made me feel better. Keep sharing your gift."

I was so touched. "I appreciate that so much," I said. "More than you know. Thank you."

As she continued down the aisle and sat behind me I couldn't help but think that she looked strangely familiar. I knew that face. And that voice. But I couldn't put my finger on it and it was driving me crazy.

Just then I heard the flight attendant ask her, "Can I get you anything, Mrs. Robinson?"

Mrs. Robinson? Huh? The only Mrs. Robinson I knew was the world's most famous cougar, the middle-aged but sexy character from the groundbreaking movie *The Graduate*. The man-hungry older woman in the black bra and matching half-slip who seduced a young Dustin Hoffman. I could picture her, smoking cigarettes in her leopard coat while shamelessly flirting with his poor, flustered character, Benjamin. *Oh, my God!*

"Call me Mrs. Brooks," she playfully told the flight attendant.

I started doing the math in my head. *Wait a minute! Mrs. Robinson, plus Mrs. Brooks, add* The Graduate, *carry the Mel Brooks, and oh my God! Yes! Mrs. Mel Brooks!* She was Academy Award–winning legend Anne Bancroft!

I mean, making *anyone* feel better made me happy, but the fact that the star of *The Miracle Worker, The Graduate, The Elephant Man, Agnes of God, 'night, Mother*, and so many other classic movies had somehow been touched by me hit me like a ton of bricks. And it also taught me that, without taking myself too seriously, what I do can help, even if it's just making one person smile. I'm proud of that.

My father died less than two weeks later and, within a year, Anne was gone, too. I'd like to think that right now maybe my father is up in heaven telling her one of his dirty jokes and making her laugh.

Elizabeth Taylor

COCKTAIL

Who's Afraid of Gin and Vermouth?

2½ ounces gin

½ ounce dry vermouth

1 dash orange bitters

1 lemon

In a glass with ice, stir the gin and vermouth for about thirty seconds. Strain into another glass, add a dash of orange bitters, and squeeze the peel of a lemon over the top so the natural oils go into the drink. Enjoy while wearing as many diamonds as you can find.

ROSSIPE

Cheese Has Always Brought Me Luck

I love a good cheese plate almost as much as I love life itself. Here are my tips to make it perfect: First, you need cheese. LOTS of cheese. Get different types—hard, soft, orange, white, mild, and stinky. Then make sure to include fruit—I love fresh grapes and blackberries, as well as some dried figs or apricots. Also, you need a variety of crackers, and just for funsies, I always include a little ramekin of honey or marmalade. Some people love nuts on their cheese plates, but I don't like them and I'm a hard nut to crack.

I once saw an interview with Barbara Walters where she revealed that Elizabeth Taylor was her worst interview ever. If nothing else, that's one thing Barbara and I have in common. Let me explain . . .

Back in December of 2002, *The Tonight Show* sent me to cover the star-studded Macy's Passport event—a big annual HIV/AIDS fundraiser fashion show hosted by living legend Sharon Stone.

I was given a list of celebrities who would be there, and it was a lot of local newspeople and reality TV stars. Now, don't get me wrong, I love both of those worlds—when I'm not watching my local news, I'm escaping from it with some much-needed, no-thinking-necessary reality TV. But as someone whose job it is to interview famous people and make an event look exciting and glamorous, I felt a little concerned as I scanned the guest list. As Bea Arthur famously said, looking around at the other guests at Pamela Anderson's Comedy Central roast, "Can someone please punch me in the face so I can see some stars?!"

Then I saw a name—THE NAME—on that list which sent my heart racing and my imagination soaring: Elizabeth Taylor!

Yes, the iconic Oscar-winning star of *National Velvet, Giant, A Place in the Sun, Cat on a Hot Tin Roof, Cleopatra*, and *Who's Afraid of Virginia Woolf?*, just to name a few. I've seen all her movies, of course, but one of my favorite Elizabeth Taylor memories may be her infamous, scene-stealing moment when she clumsily but adorably announced the 2001 Golden Globe for Best Picture in her signature sing-song (some say slightly tipsy) warble: "*Glaaadiatorrrrrrrrr!*"

But it wasn't just her undeniable star power that endeared her to the world, it was also her tireless work as a humanitarian. After all, she was one of the very first A-list celebrities to lend her valuable name and fame to bring awareness to, and fight for people with, HIV/AIDS. Wow, what a lady.

Oh, and how she loved the gays! I had heard tales of her regular trips to the Abbey—the biggest, most famous gay bar in West Hollywood. The word was that she had her very own booth there! (I've since become friends with the owner and manager of the Abbey—those rumors were true!) I'd always daydream about hanging out with her in her personal booth at the Abbey wearing matching caftans, cracking jokes, and occasionally screaming out

"*Glaaadiatorrrrrrrrr*" whenever an overly tanned and impressively muscular WeHo queen walked by.

I couldn't believe Elizabeth and I were going to be at the same event. Would I get to meet her? Just the thought gave me diarrhea tummy. I reached out to my *Tonight Show* team via email. "Umm, am I interviewing Elizabeth Taylor?"

I received a reply immediately. I was told, in no uncertain terms, that I would absolutely NOT, under any circumstances, get to interview her. The producers of the event had made it very clear: Elizabeth was NOT doing press.

Truth? I was honestly kind of relieved.

I know that may come as a bit of a surprise. You may have gathered from reading this book or watching me on TV that I am a real go-getter who seldom takes no for an answer. And, oh, honey, you're right! Not only can I usually turn lemons into lemonade, but I'll also add a shot of limoncello, a hand-carved strawberry rosette garnish, and serve it in a gorgeous vintage mid-century modern highball glass, too. You get the idea.

I pride myself on making the impossible possible. So when I was told that Elizabeth Taylor was off-limits, I normally would have taken that as a challenge and started planning a kooky *I Love Lucy*–adjacent plot to not only meet her, but end up in her lap getting the best interview of both our careers. Who could say no to this face?!

Well, *I* said no to this face. That's right. This was one of those situations when I completely agreed with what I was being told. The moment I heard the words "You will not be meeting Miss Taylor," I thought to myself, *You know what, Ross? That's probably wise. I honestly shouldn't meet her. She's too big of a star. I mean, I know I'll never interview the sun, and Elizabeth Taylor burns almost as bright, and I could get burned. Nope, this just isn't gonna happen and we're all probably better off for it.*

I put Elizabeth Taylor in the back of my mind and went to work, running around the Santa Monica Airport hangar in an outfit I'd bought just for the event (but, with time, now look back on like, "Whaaaa . . . ?"). I paired a lime-green blazer with a tangerine dress shirt. I looked like two scoops of fruit sherbet. It was the kind of outfit that made people look down to see where the extension cord was attached. Hey—don't judge me. We all make mistakes. And at the time, I thought I looked awesome.

I was interviewing someone when, out of the corner of my eye, I saw my *Tonight Show* producer. He was talking to an important-looking person I didn't recognize. It all seemed very serious, and they both kept looking over at me. Despite the less-than-exciting interview I was in the middle of, I suddenly felt a buzz in the air. Something was up. Call it intuition or Spidey sense, but I had been doing this long enough to know when something major was about to happen. Just then, my writer Anthony gave me his signal to "wrap it up," and so I quickly but gracefully thanked the person I was interviewing and headed over to Anthony who was now frantically waving me over, being about as subtle as my hideous shirt/jacket combination. I heard the PR person say, "Okay, have Ross come with me now and he can have two minutes with Elizabeth Taylor. But it has to happen *now!*"

Holy shit. To this day, I have no idea how or why the situation changed. Maybe the Gay Gods were shining down on me that day? But I didn't care. I just knew the pressure was on, it was crunch time, and I couldn't fuck this one up.

It was maybe a thirty-second walk to Elizabeth Taylor's trailer, and there was absolutely no time to think. I tried to prep questions, but what do you ask a star as giant as Elizabeth Taylor?!? Despite trying to concentrate, all I could hear was my heart throbbing in my ears.

Just before we walked inside, the publicist grabbed my arm, looked me dead in the eye, and said, "One more thing—you must refer to her as Dame Elizabeth."

I thought, *Oh yeah, just like Dame Edna! But it's not Dame Edna . . . Ross, do NOT say Dame Edna!*

I walked in and she was sitting there, totally jewel-encrusted, looking exactly like the star she was. This was all too much. There were so many lights and her little dog was barking . . .

Dame Elizabeth, NOT Dame Edna . . . Dame Elizabeth, NOT Dame Edna . . .

And then it happened. Yep, you guessed it. I mean, this plot twist is about as obvious as John Travolta's alleged hairpiece, so let's just get to it. I opened my mouth and it just came out . . .

"Dame Edna . . . lizabeth Taylor!"

Even her dog stopped barking, cocked its head, and just looked at me like, "Are you fucking kidding me, queen?"

God Dame-it. I looked around for a hole to climb into. There wasn't one. And her purse didn't look big enough to hold me, so I just took a deep breath and tried to move on.

When in doubt, compliment a person, right? It's the oldest trick in the book. I told her she looked beautiful—which was 100 percent true. She looked like the ultimate star. She was in a sparkling dress, dripping in jewels, but all of that paled in comparison to the light emanating from her world-famous lavender eyes—which were now boring into my soul. She looked at me like her dog just had: head cocked, not impressed. I could tell: Dame Elizabeth was already over me.

I was in what can only be described as "interview quicksand." I struggled to stay alive and trudged forward. This was going to work. I was going to win her over. One day we'd be in that booth at the Abbey together and look back on all of this and laugh.

"Do you like my outfit?" I asked, my already annoying voice quivering and my legs shaking.

She looked me up and down and then, after what seemed like an eternity, finally said, "Not particularly."

Of course she didn't!

I was totally rattled. This was my big moment with one of the biggest stars of all time and it was going down in flames. "Are you excited to go into the party?" I asked her. "They have an open bar in there . . . My treat!"

She just stared at me and then said, "Does that turn you on?"

Okay. I had just invited one of the world's most famous recovering alcoholics to join me at the open bar. Maybe I should bring up Debbie Reynolds or make fun of her tracheotomy scar next. It couldn't get any worse. I looked at her purse again, thinking, *You know, I bet I could fit in there if I really tried.*

And that's when the entire house of cards formerly known as my brain collapsed. I was done. I was speechless. I had nothing.

So I tried to get out of there with what little dignity I still had left by clumsily muttering barely audible half sentences as I backed out of her trailer.

"Or we can . . . Maybe we should . . ." And then, just before I went backwards out the door, I looked into those lovely lavender eyes and asked, "Are we done here?"

Right before the door slammed in my face, I heard Elizabeth Taylor say, "I think we are."

That's the worst celebrity interview I've ever done, and I think about it every time I go to the Abbey, as I daydream about how, in a different world, maybe we could've been friends. But I hold no ill will toward Dame Elizabeth. I mean, if I had to humiliate myself in front of anyone, why not swing for the stars? As the sailors in their coconut bras sing in *South Pacific*, "There is nothin' like a dame . . ."

Beyoncé

COCKTAIL

Spiked Lemonade

4 cups lemonade

2 cups club soda or sparkling water

1 cup vodka

½ cup raspberries

In a pitcher, combine lemonade, club soda, and vodka with ice. Stir and pour into a glass with raspberries in the bottom (the berries soak up the juice and are a wonderful little snack when you've finished your glass). Pour two glasses—one for you and one for Becky with the good hair.

Brekkie with the Good Haircots Verts (frittata with green beans)

Handful fresh green beans (also known as haircots verts, pronounced "hair coverts")

½ shallot, sliced

Pinch crushed red pepper

3 eggs

Salt

Chives, chopped

2 tablespoons parmesan cheese

Boil water in a saucepan and quickly blanch green beans (put them in for 20–30 seconds to quickly cook them). Remove green beans and place into a bowl with ice and water (this stops them from cooking).

In a nonstick pan (one that can also go into the oven) with just a teeny bit of olive oil, heat your sliced shallot and crushed red pepper on medium until the shallots are slightly done. Add the green beans.

In a separate bowl, mix eggs, a pinch of salt, chopped chives, and parmesan. Pour the mixture into the saucepan. Gently mix all the ingredients together and then place in an oven at 400° for 10–14 minutes, or until the middle is done.

Here's a fun fact: Did you know that Beyoncé doesn't do interviews anymore? True story. Take a moment to think about it. When is the last time you saw anybody do a good ol'-fashioned-sit down with Queen Bey? Has Diane Sawyer interviewed her lately? Nope. Tom Brokaw? Nope. Oprah? NOprah. I couldn't tell you when the last time Beyoncé sat down for an interview was, but I can tell you who was one of the last people who had the privilege of interviewing her. What's his name? You know, that gorgeous guy who talks to all the celebs? The really hot one? No, not Ryan Seacrest, you a-hole! Me! Ross William Mathews, the First.

In 2009, Jay Leno was leaving *The Tonight Show* and handing the reins over to Conan O'Brien. We all know what happened next (spoiler alert: Leno quickly got the reins back), but at the time I had no clue that we'd be back at *The Tonight Show* just a few months later, so I was looking for work elsewhere. I got a gig working freelance for *Entertainment Tonight* and its sister show, *The Insider*, covering events for them and interviewing celebrities on location and at press junkets.

A press junket is a very strange place. The stars of a movie or TV show sit sometimes for hours in a room and do tons of interviews, one after another after another, with reporters (like yours truly) entering for a quick five to seven minutes of facetime. Truth be told, I sort of hate doing press junkets. After a couple interviews, the celebrities are understandably always over it. Plus, it's such an inorganic place to have a conversation—sitting knee-to-knee in director's chairs in a random hotel room with cameras rolling. So I made it a point to not do too many of them. "I'm better in the field," I'd tell the producers.

So, after I'd quickly learned that stilted, unspontaneous press junkets weren't really my thing, for the most part they went to other correspondents. However, when the producers got wind that Beyoncé was doing press for her new movie *Obsessed*, they offered me the gig.

"Ross," the producer told me over the phone, "we've got a press junket we want you to cover. It's in New York and—"

I interrupted. "Ugh . . . a press junket? I dunno, I—"

Now the producer interrupted me. "It's Beyoncé."

Oh, well, now, that was a different story! I had been "Crazy in Love" with Beyoncé since the early Destiny's Child days, so I dropped everything and hopped on a flight to New York. This was an interesting time in Beyoncé's career—after going solo from her famous girl group, after her *I Am . . . Sasha Fierce* album, but before she achieved world domination with the undeniable masterpiece *Lemonade*. At the time, she was a huge star with unlimited potential and I was "Drunk in Love" with her. Everyone knew she was a "Survivor," but nobody really knew how much she'd grow. Not even me.

And now she was starring in *Obsessed*—not only the title of a film she was starring in but the way I felt about her! The movie was about a loyal wife (Beyoncé) whose husband is stalked by a crazy woman. I'm not going to lie to you. *Obsessed* was kinda truly awful. I mean it was fun, but I wouldn't exactly call it "quality cinema." When I saw it in the theater, the entire audience laughed—and it wasn't a comedy. Okay, I really enjoyed getting to see Beyoncé whip her weave around and kick the ass of her baby daddy's wacky would-be lover, but that was about it. It was sort of like a bad TV-movie-of-the-week version of the classic thriller *Fatal Attraction*, but much less fatal. And attractive. But as I've always said, "Bad pizza is better than no pizza," and I feel the same way about any Beyoncé projects. Like with pizza, I'm just grateful.

As I flew to New York to sit down one-on-one with the one and only Queen Bey, I started writing down some questions that would be interesting, fun, and—most important—not at all about her so-so new movie.

I remember getting to the hotel suite that day and being nervous, going over and over my questions. I was there on behalf of *The Insider* and had to wait while *Entertainment Tonight*'s Kevin Frazier interviewed Beyoncé before me. As they spoke, I hid in the bathroom and listened to make sure I didn't ask any of the same questions. At the end of his interview, Kevin asked about Jay-Z, and rather than answering his question, Beyoncé just coughed. He asked it again and, yet again, she just coughed. It was so awkward. Then I heard a publicist from Beyoncé's team whisper, "That's her new thing. She's just gonna cough whenever anyone asks about her personal life."

Oh, shit. *Okay,* I thought to myself as I scanned my prepared questions, *what am I gonna do?* Now I was really nervous. I feverishly scratched off all my questions about her family, tossing them "To the left, to the left . . ."

"Ross," my producer hollered to me, "you're up!"

When I walked out of the bathroom, the cameras were already rolling and I took my seat. Beyoncé was looking down, checking her phone, and my heart was beating out of my chest. The following is taken verbatim from the interview. You can watch it on YouTube.

"Oh!" Beyoncé looked up. She exclaimed, a huge smile now covering her face. "I love you!"

Major diaper moment. Cleanup on aisle Ross Mathews! I was elated! "Don't say it if you don't mean it!"

"I do, I do!" she replied, beaming. "I just wanna laugh. You make me happy!"

"Beyoncé!" I tried to keep it together. "You saying that makes me so happy because you know this was bound to happen one day. You and me sitting down in front of each other."

She agreed. "I know! It was bound to happen. It's this magic right here."

"Do you feel it, too?"

She did! "I feel it!"

This was going great. I had a ton of questions prepared, but this was going so well, I thought I'd try to have a little fun with her. "You may have noticed I dressed up."

"You look very handsome." She *had* noticed!

I decided to just go for it. "Thank you so much, you look gorgeous. I kind of felt like this is as close as I'd ever get to going to prom with you."

She laughed. Beyoncé laughed! And I think she liked my outfit. "Good job!"

" 'Cuz don't you think in high school we could've gone to prom?"

Again, she agreed with me! "I think so!"

Then I asked her something that was really bothering me. Well, honestly, it wasn't a big deal in the scheme of things, but it was just a personal pet peeve and I was just trying to help. "One thing I wanna know . . ." She looked at me, sincerely. I continued. "When you're singing, it's 'Beyoncé,' right? But when you're acting, it's 'Beyoncé Knowles.' But I just wanna throw this out there—Cher won an Oscar, Madonna won a Golden Globe . . . Why the double name?"

She put her hand on her face and nodded, really letting it sink in. "I think that is a great observation and I might have to drop the last name."

I was so happy to be helpful. And just to point out, when was the last time you saw her use her last name? You're welcome, world. And you can send your thank-you cards to Ross. Yes, just Ross.

After talking about getting her body in shape for the film (she does a lot of squats), I told her that I had just lost weight, too, on *Celebrity Fit Club*. "I lost weight, too, Beyoncé."

She said, "I know!"

Wow, I thought, *Beyoncé really knows who I am.* I was shocked. "You know?"

"Yes! You look great!"

Here I was a huge fan of hers and she had actually seen me on TV before. I joked, "Do you want my autograph, Beyoncé?"

She burst into laughter. "I do! I told you that I love you. I'm in love with you."

I looked around the room, asking, "Can somebody get me a pen so I can give the dear an autograph?"

We both cracked up, but then I saw her publicist giving me the "wrap up" signal. I needed to end the interview, but how? "This was a fun interview, huh?"

Beyoncé smiled. "It was so fun, as usual."

Suddenly I knew how to wrap it up. "I love you. Thanks for talking to me. And you know what, if we could turn back time, like Cher, I'd ask you to go to prom with me."

She seemed genuinely touched. "You would? And I never went to my own prom."

Unacceptable! I was shocked. "WHAT? Let's redo it!"

"Yes!" Beyoncé was in! Then she asked me, "What is our song?"

Oh, girl, that's an easy question. I knew right away. "It's gotta be a Beyoncé song. 'Halo'!"

And as I started singing one of my favorite Beyoncé songs to Beyoncé, I stood up from my chair as she stood up from hers and we hugged. As I walked out of the room, I continued to sing the entire song. What the cameras didn't catch was that Beyoncé—global superstar and Ross Mathews superfan—was singing right along with me. Now, *that's* a moment I call "Irreplaceable."

CHAPTER TWELVE

A Dollop of Dudes

COCKTAIL

MANhattan

2½ ounces bourbon

1 ounce sweet vermouth

2 dashes bitters

1 maraschino cherry

1 sprig rosemary

Combine bourbon, sweet vermouth, and bitters in a glass with ice.
Stir, add the maraschino cherry, and garnish with a sprig of fresh
rosemary. Serve in an ice-cold beer mug like a manly man.

ROSSIPE

Macho Nachos

Okay, I'm not going to try to reinvent the nachos for you. Why? Because they're already perfect, duh. But I will tell you a way to make nachos even better. I recently went to a restaurant with a group of friends and we, of course, ordered nachos. But when they came out, we were all blown away. Rather than piling the chips high on a plate, sprinkling cheese over, and putting the main ingredients on the top of the pile (I hate that because after like ten cheese-, sour cream–, and jalapeño-covered bites, you're left with a pile of dry tortilla chips), this restaurant put the chips on a big baking sheet and spread the ingredients all over so every bite was perfect. GAME CHANGER! I know what you're thinking: "Ross, that's nacho idea . . ."

WOW, THAT WAS a whole lotta ladies! But what can I say? They love me! Chicks, am I right? But now it's time to butch this book up a li'l bit. Yeah, lemme mansplain something to you real quick: Every once in a while a guy's gotta "bro out" and have some good ol' male bonding, bud. So without further ado, come with me now into my man cave, sit in that La-Z-Boy recliner, fart, scratch your balls, and meet some of my boys, dude. (Be honest, I can't pull this off, can I?)

Mr. T

COCKTAIL

Mr. T Sweet Tea

¾ cup brewed tea of your choice (I like a fruit tea)

⅓ cup whiskey

3 tablespoons simple syrup

1 lemon

Combine tea, whiskey, and simple syrup in a shaker with ice. Use your big manly muscles to shake vigorously for 30 seconds. Strain into a glass. Squeeze ¼ of a lemon into the drink and garnish with a lemon slice.

ROSSIPE

Steamed Muscly Mussels

2 pounds fresh mussels, cleaned

1½ tablespoons butter

Pinch crushed red pepper

1 large shallot, thinly sliced

3 cloves garlic, thinly sliced

Salt and pepper, to taste

1 cup chicken stock

½ cup white wine

1 lemon

Handful chopped parsley

1 loaf of really good bread (I love sourdough)

First, clean your fresh mussels. Here's how. Soak them in a bowl of fresh cool water. Then rinse them and use a brush to scrub them, removing as many fibers as possible. Throw away any that are chipped or cracked.

Melt butter in a large pot over medium heat. Once butter is melted, stir in a pinch of crushed red pepper, thinly sliced shallots and garlic, as well as a dash of salt and pepper (you can always add more later). Stir for a few minutes, and then add chicken stock, white wine, and cleaned mussels. Toss a bit, and then cover for 6–10 minutes. If a mussel doesn't open, toss it—it's no good. Stir in chopped parsley and serve with a big slice of bread.

I pity the fool who doesn't know who Mr. T is. Back in the 1980s, thanks to roles in movies like *Rocky III* and the hit TV show *The A-Team*, Mr. T was a mega-buff mega-superstar! With his signature mohawk, gold chains, and booming, gruff voice, he was like a real-life cartoon character. Oh, and he actually was a cartoon character, too! And, as if that weren't enough, he had his own cereal, too! I used to eat bowl after bowl of his sugary corn puffs shaped into Ts while watching the animated version of him stomp around, telling kids to stay off drugs and coming to the rescue time and time again. I've never been 100 percent sure, but as far as I'm concerned, the T in Mr. T probably stands for "Terrific!"

So you can just imagine my shock and delight the day I saw the real Mr. T—in the flesh—standing an arm's length away from me. But, before you get too excited, this story doesn't have a happy ending. Let me spill the Mr. T tea . . .

It was 2002 in New York City, and I was covering the red carpet at NBC's 75th Anniversary Party for *The Tonight Show*. Seventy-five years is what they call the Diamond Anniversary. Can I quickly just ask who "they" are? What mysterious people decided this? Is it the same people who dictate such things like Unspoken Salad Bar Etiquette and Not Making Eye Contact in an Elevator? If so, I'd like to meet them. I mean, diamonds are great, but if it were up to me the seventy-fifth anniversary would be the Miniature Pony Anniversary. Hello! Diamonds may be forever, but you can't dress a diamond up like a cute li'l unicorn and ride it! Now *that's* a party!

But even without a pony, this NBC 75th Anniversary was an amazing party. Absolutely everyone was there. It was like the little portable Panasonic TV (with the wire-hanger antenna) from my childhood bedroom had thrown up and there were stars of yesteryear everywhere! We're talking television titans like cast members from NBC's *Cheers, Friends, Frasier, ER,* and *The Cosby Show* (back when we could still enjoy it). And the two cherries on this star-studded sundae? A double dose of *Golden Girls* grandma glamour, Betty White and Rue McClanahan!

My head was twisting and turning like a possessed ventriloquist dummy . . . on a roller coaster . . . DURING AN EARTHQUAKE! Okay, you get it.

After interviewing almost everyone there, I was exhausted and getting ready to pack up and leave when I suddenly saw—out of the corner of my eye—something glint from across the room.

I turned to see that it was a giant diamond stud in the earlobe of my favorite childhood cartoon character (if you don't count *Jem and the Holograms*): Mr. T! It was flashing at me like a beacon, like a nearly six-foot-tall muscle-bound lighthouse with a mohawk.

As I excitedly skipped over to him with even more spring in my step than usual, I saw that he was taking a photo surrounded by a group of fans with his back to me. I waited patiently, knowing in my heart that this was going to be a moment I would never forget. Boy, was I right.

When they were done taking photos, I made my approach. I cleared my throat, politely tapped him on the shoulder, and sweetly chirped, "Excuse me, Mr. T?"

This next part happened in slow motion. As he turned around, before even seeing me, he sweetly asked, in the most boisterous and warm way possible, "How can I help you, little lady?" with a giant smile on his famous face.

Then time stopped. Awkward!

The moment he took one look at me, that beaming smile immediately collapsed, morphing into that weird emoji with a straight line for a mouth. Obviously the voice he had just heard and the face he had just seen, in his mind, didn't go together at all. He stared at me blankly as if to say, "DOES NOT COMPUTE." I just blinked. We both froze—speechless—and then, as if we were two malfunctioning robots, slowly turned away at the same time and walked in opposite directions.

At that moment I'm pretty sure the T in Mr. T stood for "Terrified."

But Mr. T, if you're reading this (and I just assume you are), don't worry—we're all good. It takes a lot more than a little mis-

understanding like that to make me change my mind about one of my childhood heroes. You're still A-Team to me. Don't worry, I still am, and always will be . . .

All Mr. T, no shade.

Matt LeBlanc

COCKTAIL

Sauvignon LeBlanc

A nice crisp bottle of Italian Sauvignon Blanc.

ROSSIPE

Pigs in a LeBlancket

Premade pastry dough

Dijon mustard

Mini kosher dill pickles, sliced

Mini sausages or hot dogs

Ketchup

Sriracha

Unroll premade pastry dough. Cut dough into squares if it's not already perforated. Squirt a dollop of Dijon mustard and place slice of dill pickle on each square. Then place a small sausage or hot dog (your choice) on top and roll the dough around it. Place

on a baking sheet lined with parchment paper and cook at 350°
for 12–15 (until golden brown).

While they bake, mix two parts ketchup with one part Sriracha in
a small bowl.

When the Pigs in a LeBlancket are done, allow to cool, dip into the
spicy ketchup, and share with your *Friends*.

At the same event where I met Mr. T, I also interviewed the two Matts—LeBlanc and Perry—from NBC's mega-hit must-see sitcom *Friends*. You know, for two guys on a show called *Friends*, they were anything but friendly to me. As a matter of fact, if I were an NBC executive I would have probably named the show *Jerks*.

As I mentioned before, all the NBC stars were out to celebrate that night for the network's seventy-fifth anniversary, and I was beyond excited to interview all of them on the red carpet. Normally on red carpets, among countless other media outlets, it's survival of the fittest. You scream for their attention, you plead, you beg. So basically, it's like going on a first date with me. But since this was an NBC event and I was holding a big *Tonight Show* microphone, they all came directly over to talk to me. I felt like the hottest girl at prom! I gabbed with television icons like George Wendt, who had played Norm on *Cheers*; Don Adams, who had played Agent Maxwell Smart on *Get Smart*; Barbara Eden, who had played Jeannie on *I Dream of Jeannie*, just to name a few.

But I was most excited to meet and interview the stars of NBC's comedy crown jewel and my personal favorite TV show, *Friends*. And I wasn't alone—each week, between twenty to thirty million people would tune in to see if Rachel would end up with Ross or if Chandler would marry Monica, or if that dumb monkey Marcel would finally be written off the show (sorry, but I never got that monkey business).

Kids today won't understand, but no TV show gets those kinds of ratings now. Must See TV was what everyone watched (hence the name) and discussed the next day. This was before streaming and bingeing. You had to wait a whole week to see what was going to happen next. The only thing streaming were the tears of laughter running down my cheeks, and the only bingeing was me on Totino's Pizza Rolls. It was huge, I was huge, and I was there for it every single week.

So you can only imagine my sheer, unadulterated excitement when Matthew Perry and Matt LeBlanc approached me. Chandler Bing and Joey Tribbiani themselves! I knew for certain this was gonna be great! After all, I loved them on TV, they were funny, and I was a big fan. What could possibly go wrong?

This interview is actually on YouTube. I found it as I was writing this story, and it is as painful to watch as it felt that night so long ago. Maybe more so.

As they approached, fans were screaming and the chaos of the red carpet was at a fever pitch. Excitedly—admittedly, perhaps a little *too* excitedly—I squealed at the top of my lungs, "It is so great to meet you! I'm Ross!"

Matt LeBlanc replied, "No you're not, he's over there" as he motioned toward his costar David Schwimmer (who played the character Ross on *Friends*).

Good! I thought. *They're here to play!*

"Oh, yeah, the other Ross," I replied, jokingly rolling my eyes. That didn't go over well. Immediately the mood changed.

Matthew Perry began staring into the camera blankly as Matt LeBlanc asked, "How did you get this gig?"

I could feel things going wrong. "I slept my way to the top."

It was a lame comeback, but I was suddenly so nervous. Matthew Perry continued to deadpan into the camera, ignoring me.

At that time I hadn't been doing red carpets long, so I guess I expected them to be like their fun-loving characters on TV. They were not that. Instead, my enthusiasm hit a brick wall.

Rather than replying to me, Matt LeBlanc pointed to me, then looked into the camera, and said "Jay, are you kidding? Are you kidding, Jay?"

Matthew Perry joined in, addressing the camera and asking, "What's the call here, Jay?"

I remember thinking *What the fuck is their problem?*, but of course I didn't say that. I did say, though, "Are you guys kidding? Rude to my face?"

But I tried to steer the interview back on track. Even this early into my career, I knew I had to get a good segment for the show. Plus, growing up in a farm town I was sort of used to being mocked by arrogant straight guys who thought I was some sort of joke. As a result, I was very good at pretending like this sort of thing didn't bother me. So, as I had done so many times before, I just plastered a smile on my face, bulldozed ahead, and tried to make lemonade out of these two lemons. Very Beyoncé, very ahead of my time.

I tried to salvage the interview with a softball question: "Are you gonna be at the after party?"

Matthew Perry replied, looking into camera again, referencing me, "Jay, this is not long-term thinking."

As they walked away, I looked into the camera. "I think I bugged them."

Just like the iconic theme song says, "So no one told you life was gonna be this way. Your job's a joke, you're broke, that interview was DOA . . . CLAP CLAP CLAP CLAP."

Whatever. I chalked it all up to a bad night and went on with my life.

Cut to fifteen years later. I was on the red carpet for the SAG Awards, interviewing the stars as they arrived for E! During a commercial break, I felt a tap on my shoulder. It was Matt LeBlanc. I hadn't seen him since our beyond awkward encounter all those years earlier.

I hadn't even thought of our interaction since it happened, but the minute he said hello, it all came flooding back to me. I had no clue what he wanted. I was suddenly on edge. He seemed oddly nervous, too. "Hey, man. It's good to see you."

"You, too." There was a palpable heaviness in the air.

"Look," he said, taking a breath, "I don't know if you even remember this, but years ago you interviewed me on a red carpet and I was really rude to you. It's bugged me ever since and I've always wanted to apologize to you. It wasn't cool of me to do that to you. I'm sorry."

I tried to process everything he was saying, but it was during a commercial break of our live broadcast, I had a producer talking in my ear, and I was being pulled in a million different directions. So, in the frenzy of everything going on, rather than tell him how much his apology meant to me, I just sort of brushed it off. "Oh, don't even worry about it. I don't even remember that. Good to see you! Bye!"

After the live broadcast, I finally had some time to process what Matt had said. It was kind and gracious and honestly shocking to me that he had felt that way for so long. Despite what I had just told him, the truth was that I did remember every detail of our first encounter and I had held on to it. It had even ruined the final season of *Friends* for me. There weren't enough Totino's Pizza Rolls in the world to fill that pain.

When Matt said he was sorry, I wish I had handled it differently. I wish I had been able to tell him what it meant to me. And if I had to do it over again, I would have told him that it did hurt me back then. That he did make me feel like I didn't belong. That he did make me worry that my bosses would think I was bad at my job. That I didn't want my mom to see it. And that, after all these years, the fact that he told me he was sorry meant a lot to me. I didn't know how much I'd needed to hear that.

If I never get to tell you that in person, Matt, now you know. Thanks.

Your move, Matthew Perry.

Jason Priestley

COCKTAIL

Peach Pit Punch

1½ cups rum

2 12-ounce cans ginger ale

1 lime

Fresh (or canned) peaches

Fresh mint

In a pitcher, mix rum, ginger ale, the juice of 1 lime, and peaches with ice. Serve with a fresh mint garnish.

9021-Olive Tapenade

1 loaf of good bread

2 tablespoons olive oil

1 cup pitted Kalamata olives

3 garlic cloves

2 tablespoons fresh lemon juice

Handful fresh parsley

Salt and pepper, to taste

Slice bread, brush with olive oil, and place on a baking sheet in an oven at 400° for 3–5 minutes, until toasted.

Place olives, garlic, lemon juice, olive oil, and parsley into a blender. Pulse until it's all finely chopped. Pour into a bowl and salt and pepper to taste. Serve with toasted bread on the side.

I'm not very good at remembering anything—when Easter is, what my blood type is, what my password for Uber Eats is— but I do know the zip code for a very expensive, very exclusive neighborhood here in Los Angeles that I will probably never live in. Yes, thanks to whoever argued that it should be a part of the title of a new TV show starring a gaggle of unknown but good-looking teenagers, I—and everyone else on this planet—knows the zip code for Beverly Hills: 90210.

Growing up, I loved the TV show *Beverly Hills, 90210* so much. For teens during the 1990s it was *the* show to watch. We all wanted to be like the teenagers on that show—spoiled, rich, and gorgeous. I was none of those things, but for an hour every week I got to pretend that I was one of the cool kids, too.

Every Wednesday night I'd sit my poor ugly ass down to watch the rich gorgeous people in the *Nine-Oh/Melrose Place* block while on the phone with my friend Andrea. Let me explain something to you, kids . . . Back in the day, we had something called a "landline." This line terminated in a large, bulky contraption on which you could communicate with friends, or call in sick to your minimum wage job when Madonna was performing on the Oscars. It had a very long cord that allowed one to get a snack in the kitchen, let the dog out into the backyard, and even visit the bathroom while still yapping with a friend. Later, we would get a fancy schmancy "cordless phone," which resembled a small kitchen appliance with a big antenna on it. Thanks to this groundbreaking technology, one could literally walk out the front door and keep talking on the phone while getting the mail—just so long as the mailbox was no more than fifteen feet or so from the house.

When I was in middle school, it was not uncommon for me and Andrea to spend hours on the phone, watching TV "together." Nowadays a person would never dream of calling a friend without texting them and making an appointment first. When my iPhone rings now, I look at it like a toddler seeing his reflection for the first time: "Whaaaa?"

Every Wednesday night Andrea and I would be on the phone

for *two hours* watching the teen drama *Beverly Hills, 90210* and then the much racier *Melrose Place* (which featured a gay character, which was groundbreaking, even though he never really had a storyline, let alone a love interest, but whatever—it was the nineties and I was grateful).

My small town was a world away from Beverly Hills, and despite fantasizing about being a part of their clique, I never really thought I'd ever get to meet any of the *90210* cast members in real life, but I did. I really, truly did! I met Brandon Walsh himself, Jason Priestley. I could have just died! And I also may have kinda accidentally almost caused him to die, too. Whoopsies! Let me explain . . .

One of my first big assignments as a correspondent for *The Tonight Show* was to cover the 2002 Winter Olympics in Salt Lake City. For the entire duration of the games, I was on TV every night reporting via satellite back to Jay in the NBC Burbank Studios. Suddenly, people really began to know who I was. It was exciting, if not slightly terrifying. On the way home from the games, it seemed like everyone in the Salt Lake airport knew who I was. That took some getting used to.

What didn't take getting used to was the first class lounge. All the free soda, pita chips, and chunks of cheddar cheese that I could eat. I remember thinking, *Wowzah, rich people have it made!*

There I was in the first class lounge getting my third free refill of Diet Coke when these guys with long hair came up to me. With their tattoos and ripped jeans, they seemed almost as out of place as I must have. "Hey, man!" one of them said, whipping his long hair out of his eyes. "We saw you on TV! You're so funny."

"Thanks so much!" These hobos sure seemed nice. I asked why they were in town.

"We were performing in the Olympic Medals Plaza."

I was confused. "Performing?" I asked, stuffing another cheddar chunk in my mouth. *Were they mimes? A modern dance troupe? Part of* Stars on Ice? I had to find out. "Like, what kind of performing?"

They kind of laughed. "Our music, man."

"Oh, you're in a band? Cute!" They thought that was hilarious. One good thing about being known for being funny is that people just think you're joking when you're really just an idiot.

"My name's Johnny. You're fucking funny, man."

We exchanged numbers and all made plans to hang out. Before I walked away, I asked their band name so I could look them up.

Johnny laughed. "We're the Goo Goo Dolls."

I had never heard of them. When I got back to my crew and told them, they freaked out. "Ross, they're HUGE!"

Really? I had no clue. In my defense, I was more Pussycat Dolls than Goo Goo Dolls. My coworkers played me some of their songs. One was called "Slide." Right away, I knew it. "OMG, THAT'S THEM?!?!?!?"

I was mortified. They played me more, and each song was more familiar than the last. I slapped my head into my palms. *Ross,* I thought, *you're a fucking fool.*

So, despite that rather embarrassing first meeting, a friendship quickly blossomed among me, Goo Goo Dolls' lead singer Johnny Rzeznick, and bass player Robby Takac. We would go out to dinner and try to talk while frenzied female fans approached them asking for autographs or to take a picture or to have them father their children. At one point, one of us had a crazy idea—I can't remember who: What if I went on the road with them and filmed it for a *Tonight Show* segment? Everyone—including my producers—thought it was a great idea, so we made it happen.

In mid-August of 2002, I headed to Cincinnati to meet up with the Dolls (their *real* friends always drop the "Goo Goo" when referring to them!) on one of their tour dates. I was waiting at the ticket counter to check in for an early morning flight when a very good-looking guy in a flannel shirt got in line behind me. Take note: It's *never* too early to check someone out. I looked like I had just rolled out of bed (which I had), but this guy was wearing a stylish hat, cool sunglasses, and was rocking some serious sideburns. Yeah, it was a major look. And it was working for him. As I started to walk away from the counter, in desperate need of some Starbucks, he stepped up and handed the lady his ID. "Hello, Mr. Priestley . . ." the agent said, somehow managing to sound simultaneously flirty yet professional.

9021-OH-MY-GOD. I didn't know what to do, but I knew I had a flight to catch, so it was suddenly a Sophie's Choice moment: I could either choose my career or make my lifelong dream of joining the Walsh family come true. I immediately started daydreaming about being adopted by Mr. and Mrs. Walsh and moving to the most famous zip code in the world. I would wear preppy Izod polo shirts in various sherbert colors with the collars popped and a sweater tied around my shoulders. Despite the fact that they were rich and had a giant house, I would have to share a room with my new stepbrother Brandon. You guys, can I ask you a question? Would it be weird to slow dance to Boyz II Men's "I'll Make Love to You" with my own stepbrother? I mean, we're not actually related and it's just a dance . . .

Just as my fantasy was about to go somewhere that would be totally inappropriate for this family-friendly book, I heard them announcing over the PA system that my flight was boarding. I didn't even have time to get a Starbucks let alone chat up my ultimate teenage crush, Jason Priestley.

I boarded my flight, sat in my window seat, and started flipping through the pile of trashy tabloids I always travel with. As I was reading a particularly juicy story, I heard someone say, "Hey man," as he extended his hand to shake mine. "I'm Jason."

I looked up. It was Him. I reached out with my trembling, sweaty hand and shook his. I honestly couldn't fathom that this was really happening. *I'm touching Jason Priestley.* Could this get any better?

He looked down at his boarding pass, and then at me, smiling. "I'm next to you, neighbor," he said as he threw his carry-on baggage into the overhead bin and sat down next to me.

If only there was a place to store my emotional baggage. MY FUCKING SEATMATE WAS JASON FUCKING PRIESTLEY.

Now, I don't know for sure if there's a God. No one really knows for sure, but there have certainly been signs: a gorgeous sunrise, how the moon pulls the tide, that new ice cream that's only 100 calories per serving. And having Jason Priestley randomly seated next to you on a four-hour flight? Now, *that's* proof that God is real!

I tried to keep my eyes forward, so as not to creep him out. But I was losing it. As we were putting our seats in their full and upright position and stowing our tray tables for takeoff, he turned to me and asked, "You're Ross, right?"

OMG! Brandon Walsh knows my name. What world am I living in?

"Yes. Ross. That's me. Ross."

The words came out of me like I was just beginning to learn English, and I was nervously nodding my head way too much.

"So great to meet you!" He was smiling. *I loved his smile.*

". . . Great to meet you," I responded.

"It's a beautiful morning, huh?" he said, looking out the window.

"Yes, it's a beautiful morning," I agreed, figuring that if I just kept repeating whatever he said, I'd be fine.

He was handling this situation much better than I was, but of course he wasn't sitting next to Jason Priestley. He *was* Jason Priestley! He asked, "Why are you going to Cincinnati?"

Huh? Cincinnati? Oh, yeah. I had forgotten why I was going. I had forgotten where I even *was.* I had forgotten *who* I was. All I knew was that I was having a conversation with Jason Priestley, it was my turn to talk, and I suddenly couldn't remember why I was on this plane in the first place.

Pull it together! It took every ounce of strength to focus. "I'm headed to meet up with the Goo Goo Dolls on tour for a *Tonight Show* segment."

"Awesome! I know those guys. They're great. I'm headed there for a race."

A race? Oh, that's right, I thought, *I forgot that he races cars now!*

After *Beverly Hills, 90210,* Jason had followed his passion for car racing and begun a successful career as a circuit racer. As my heart was racing, he continued, "It's a track outside of Cincinnati. How long are you gonna be there? You should come out and watch!"

Ummmm yes. "I will absolutely do that if I can."

He took out his cell phone. "Great, give me your number and I'll call you with the details."

After several attempts—*WHAT'S MY PHONE NUMBER, DAMMIT!?*—I finally gave him my digits.

We spent the rest of the flight talking about everything from our families to work. We even discovered that we had quite a few mutual friends in common. By the end of the flight it dawned on me that I was no longer merely starstruck, but rather struck with the fact that he was actually a really nice guy.

When we landed in Cincinnati, we said our goodbyes and I went straight to work (well, if you can call hanging out with a bunch of cute rock stars "work"). I met up with the band, and we shot for two days on the road, behind the scenes and on their tour bus. It was a blast! In fact, we got all the footage we needed ahead of schedule, so my producers decided to pack up early. They changed our flights and we all headed home.

I was bummed that we didn't stay long enough for me to go see Jason race. Truth be told, he hadn't called me, so I figured it was just one of those things celebrities do in the moment. Maybe he was just being nice. Maybe it was just an impulse. You know, like when you're watching one of those infomercials at 3 a.m. and you order that frying pan that an army tank could drive over and not ruin? And then the bill comes and, as much as you love the pan—and the fact that even burnt cheese easily wipes right off of it with just a paper towel—you kinda regret it?

Maybe Jason had the best intentions but then, looking at my number, rethought everything and just couldn't hit DIAL. But it was okay. As much as I would have loved to have seen Jason race and continue our male bonding, I was really happy to be home. Well, sort of home. I had just graduated college and didn't have a place to live yet, so I was staying in a hotel next to Universal Studios. Hello, room service!

When I awoke the next morning, I checked my cell phone and saw a voicemail from about an hour earlier. As I listened to the voicemail, I turned on the morning news in my hotel room. What happened next was shocking. Simultaneously, I soaked in both the voicemail and the TV:

VOICEMAIL: "Hey, Ross. It's Jason Priestley here. I'm at a race track just outside of Cincinnati . . ."

TELEVISION: "Breaking news: Television star Jason Priestly is in grave condition after crashing during test runs in a race track just outside of Cincinnati, Ohio . . ."

VOICEMAIL: ". . . I'm doing a few test runs before the race. Lemme know if you're still in town and want to come out to watch . . ."

TELEVISION: ". . . Priestly is currently in critical condition . . ."

VOICEMAIL: ". . . I'll keep an eye out for you, so just lemme me know. Talk soon, man. . ."

(CLICK)

TELEVISION: ". . . But reports are that the crash was very serious . . ."

I didn't know what to do. I paced back and forth in the hotel room, listening to the voicemail over and over again while glued to the news on TV. Thankfully, after surgeries and a rather difficult recovery, Jason was fine (and good news—still hot!).

I've never heard from him again, but I've always hoped to bump into him. I wonder if he even remembers meeting me. For a while, I thought maybe he'd call again, but I assume one of two things happened, but quite possibly both—his cell phone was crushed in the accident and/or he suffered a very specific type of amnesia that made him forget everyone named Ross that he met on the plane the days leading up to the accident. That could explain it, right?

But, no matter what, no one can ever take away from me the fact that for one brief moment at thirty thousand feet all those years ago, I was totally BFFs with the coolest kid at West Beverly High. And you just know that Andrea Zuckerman is soooooo jealous. She always had a crush on him. Sorry, girl, but you're just friends! Get a clue!

CHAPTER THIRTEEN

You Are Cordially Invited to My Fantasy Celebrity Dinner Party

COCKTAIL

Fantasy Fizz

---

2 ounces gin

¾ ounces simple syrup

1 lemon

Club soda

Combine gin, simple syrup, and the juice of ¼ of the lemon into a shaker with ice. Shake, then strain into a glass with ice and fill to the top with club soda.

Bunka's Famous Lemon Bars

CRUST

2 cubes butter

½ cup powdered sugar

2 cups flour

Dash salt

FILLING

4 eggs, beaten

2 cups sugar

¼ cup flour

6 tablespoons fresh lemon juice

Combine ingredients for crust, mix well, and press into a greased 9 x 3 pan. Bake at 350° for 14 minutes. Allow to cool.

While the crust is baking, mix ingredients for the filling, then pour over cooled crust and continue to bake at 350 ° for 25 minutes. When finished, allow to cool, and dust with more powdered sugar.

NOW THAT YOU'VE read my greatest celebrity stories where every word is true, it's time for me to share with you something different. Open your mind and prepare to go along with me as I take you on a journey. The following never happened. Yet. But the dream is very much alive. What you're about to read is a glimpse into the depths of my imagination. Here is, in my opinion, the perfect fantasy celebrity dinner party.

The perfect dinner party is one of life's greatest achievements. The key ingredients to creating the ideal get-together are simple: combine charming guests, delicious food, throw in a parlor game or two (like charades or Twister), shake well, and voilà!

Nirvana with napkin rings! Paradise with poached pears! Heaven with honey baked ham! Sounds simple, right? Think again, rookie.

If the delicate balance of wining, dining, mixing, and mingling was that easy to achieve, domestic goddess Martha Stewart wouldn't have built the empire she has today. Rather, "Melon Baller"—which is what I'd like to think they called Martha when she was in prison—would probably just be an assistant manager at the Bed Bath & Beyond in Burbank. (God, I *just* remembered that I have like seventeen of those 20 percent off coupons that are about to expire! Mental note!)

Yes, Martha Stewart is the undisputed high priestess of hospitality, but it's always been a secret goal of mine to momentarily knock her off her throne, at least in my own home. You know, just once wouldn't we all really love to "out Martha" Martha? She's in the back of my mind with every recipe I try and every art project I never finish. I can feel her judging me from afar, burning into my soul like a hot glue gun. It would be amazing to do something better than her, whether it was simply icing a cake or creating something crafty that she never thought of before. Sure, Martha wouldn't even know it, but I would.

The truth? I have actually met Martha Stewart on not one but two occasions. My first encounter with her was when we were both guests on an episode of *The View* in 2006. I stood mere inches away from her backstage, but she was too busy fiddling with her muffins to notice me. Sadly, that's not a metaphor. She was literally arranging her baked-to-perfection baked goods. Besides, I wouldn't have even dreamt of bothering her. She's a big deal; a real game changer. I mean, let's give credit where credit is due. If it weren't for dear, sweet, anal-retentive Martha, most people's idea of "entertaining" would still be boxed wine and pigs in a blanket. Yes, I'm looking at you, Mom. (And if you ever stop serving either of those to me, I will disown you!)

My second Martha experience was more intense. VH1 asked me to be a guest on the Halloween episode of their hit show *Martha & Snoop's Potluck Dinner Party*. I, of course, dressed as a giant purple unicorn because . . . why wouldn't I? I was thrilled to finally be blessed with some precious one-on-one face time with Martha. And you know what I learned? She's pretty much a gay man: sassy, funny as hell, and surprisingly, a little raunchy. What's not to love, right? And she certainly has no problem speaking her mind. During a commercial break, when the subject of Donald Trump and Russia came up (the first of these a man with whom she has an infamous ongoing feud), I asked her, "Oh, yeah, how do you think that's gonna end?"

Without skipping a beat, Martha said, "Oh, that fool? He's so screwed. The kindest thing that could happen to him is if he just dropped dead from a heart attack."

Snap! Okay, girl . . . All right, back to my fantasy celebrity shindig.

Let's face it, throwing a proper dinner party is really freakin' complicated. By far, the most difficult aspect is figuring out who—and more importantly, who NOT—to invite. Oh, please. I know I'm not the only person who's thought about this. Haven't you ever been at happy hour when one of your especially inquisitive friends asked you, "If you could invite anyone—living or dead—to a fantasy dinner party, who would it be?"

I take this kind of question very seriously. And I've thought a lot about it. Probably too much.

For starters, I would NOT invite any dead celebrities. Guhross. This is a dinner party, not a Halloween party, honey! And as tempting as it might be to seat Albert Einstein next to Anna Nicole Smith and watch the sparks fly (*OMG, are they gonna fight or make out?!?*), I would refrain from "playing God" by bringing famous people back from the grave so they could discuss the current state of pop music over a bowl of butternut squash soup.

I would, however, stop and ask myself, "WWJDIHWTAFDP?," which, of course, stands for, "What Would Jesus Do If He Was Throwing A Fabulous Dinner Party?" Duh.

No, I wouldn't turn water into wine like Jesus did (and honestly, who needs to with the deals you can get on bulk booze at Costco), but I would invite the same number of guests that Jesus hosted at perhaps the most famous dinner party of them all, the Last Supper: Twelve. The more the merrier, right? Plus, this is the one chance I'd get to finally use that table-expanding leaf thingy that came with my dining room set!

Okay, so enough stalling. It's time to actually choose the guests for my fantasy dinner party. Word of warning, though? If your name does not appear on this list, please DO NOT be upset with me. And more important, please DO NOT crash the party. Security will be tighter than the faces of the Real Housewives, and I will not hesitate to throw you out (but I will totally send you off with a doggie bag because I couldn't bear seeing you leave empty-handed).

I present to you the most exclusive VIP list since the heyday of Studio 54. But unlike at that famous discotheque, instead of snorting lines from a heaping mountain of coke, my guests will be forming lines at my refreshing fountain of Diet Coke. Congratulations to the following people:

My Mom

This mama's boy would never forgive himself if he didn't invite the most important lady in his life. If you think about it, there wouldn't be a party *at all* if it weren't for her. The woman carried me for nine months, so the least I could do is invite her to my fake dinner party. She'd not only help me fold the linen napkins into fancy origami-like shapes and sculpt radishes into roses but her presence would keep me grounded while I was surrounded by the crème de la crème of the world's glitterati! You know, people like . . .

Bunka

That's what I call my grandma. Yep, I'm not just a mama's boy, I'm a mama's mama's boy! I realize that "Bunka" sounds like some sort of card game a con man on the streets of Brooklyn might play to bilk unsuspecting suckers outta their hard-earned money, but that's what we call her, okay? It's been her nickname since I was six years old because my little cousin Karla couldn't say "Grandma," and it was cute, so it stuck. Bunka would score an invite to my party not only for her sparkling personality but because the woman can cook like nobody's business. I would insist that she whip up her legendary Swedish meatballs (even better than the ones they serve in the Ikea cafeteria!) and my favorite—her not-too-tart, not-too-sweet famous lemon bars. Each one is a mouthful of sunshine that she's been perfecting since the 1940s. Screw those uppity big city hipster desserts like Elderflower Gelato with Fig Foam on Agave-Crusted Flax Seed Crostini, Bunka's old-school treats are retrolicious!

Richard Simmons

The only thing that could lure the most reclusive and famous fitness fanatic out of hiding is, of course, my fantasy dinner party. And after having read the artery-clogging ingredients in Bunka's lemon bars, I'm sure you understand my need to have a voice of reason in attendance. Should I feel the uncontrollable urge to reach for a second helping of my ancestors' signature starchy crack, my maharajah of moderation, Richard, could simply give me a look from across the table, kick his tanned, glistening leg in the air, and belt out, "Step away from the side dish, sonny!"

The only thing shorter than Richard's BeDazzled shorts is his patience for overindulging. It's Richard's firm-but-loving (and firm-*butt*-loving!) guidance that ensures I'm able to button my fantasy dinner party ensemble, a vintage oxblood-red velvet smoking jacket with matching slacks right out of Hugh Hefner's walk-in closet. It's a classic, timeless look that doesn't really pack the same punch when you're packin' pudge in your pants. Plus, you never know what direction this dinner party will go, and if we all end up playing strip poker or going skinny-dipping, I don't want to feel bloated. And if things got really bad and we all really overate, he could also lead us all in a much-needed after-dinner Sweatin' to the Oldies aerobics class.

Lady Gaga

Now that Gaga and I are total besties, she'd be furious if I didn't invite her. Plus, every dinner party should have its own soundtrack, which is why I would invite the best of the best, Miss Stefani Germanotta, to join us. Just imagine her "tickling the ivories" on the white baby grand piano in my living room (and while I'm fantasizing, that piano would be conveniently located right between a frozen yogurt machine and a cluster of those fancy massage chairs from Brookstone). Of course, I would call Gaga beforehand and diplomatically explain that the dinner party dress code was classy/casual. This means no Saturn-like rings or broken shards of mirror, and absolutely no raw meat. But let's be honest, asking Gaga to tone it down is like asking me to do a James Earl Jones impersonation. Truth be told, I don't really care what Gaga wears just so long as she brings her Oscar to use as the centerpiece for my dinner table. Oh, you know Martha Stewart is kicking herself right now for not thinking of that idea for a centerpiece before me! GENIUS! Point for Mathews! Your move, Stewart!

Justin Timberlake

Every dinner party needs a little eye candy, and I have quite the sweet tooth for Mr. Timberlake. Not to sugarcoat it, but I'd love to Willy his Wonka, if you know what I mean. Break me off a piece of *that* Kit Kat bar! That's one M&M that could melt in my mouth *and* in my hand! Yeah, I said it! I've been crushin' on JT since high school, and it's about time we shared a meal together! Justin would sit right next to me at the table and would laugh at all my jokes, whether they were funny or not. You know, jokes like "Hey Justin, when you're done eating, don't worry about cleaning up—just put your dishes *NSYNC. OMG GET IT?!?"
He would totally laugh at that.

Kathie Lee Gifford

I've adored Kathie Lee for as long as I can remember! She's such a refreshingly free spirit, and I really think her zany energy would help keep the party upbeat, light, and—okay, who am I kidding? I'd invite her for one reason and one reason only: in the hopes that she'd drink a little too much and entertain us the way she entertained America for all those years during the fourth hour of *The Today Show*. I'm a sucker for a tipsy gal in her fifties. And even though I'm banking on the fact that K-Lee will no doubt guzzle several goblets of her precious Chardonnay and start dancing on the table to the delight of all my guests, I do have my limits and would have to draw the line somewhere. If neces-

205

sary, I'd have no problem pulling her aside and hissing through clenched teeth, "Listen lady, Costco closes at nine and we're running out of wine! So unless you're willing to Uber it there to buy more, slow down on the sauce, sister! And don't think for one second I can't see you playing footsies under the table with Justin. I'll admit, I like your style, honey. But if you keep it up, no dessert for you! And just so you know, I'm serving my Bunka's homemade lemon bars and they're AMAZING. And if you're good, I'll give you a corner piece. Got it? What, no snippy comeback like you always have for Hoda? Cat got your tongue? Lemme guess, it's a cougar."

Rachel Maddow

At this point, you're probably thinking I'm just a shallow person who only wants to start drama with morning talk show legends or rub elbows (and God knows what else) with gorgeous former boy band members. Well, you're wrong. I offer Exhibit A: Rachel Maddow. This no-nonsense newscaster would make sure that we discussed important topics like, umm, boring "newsy" kinda stuff. The moment my guests arrived and saw her signature simple black blazer, they would know that this wasn't just some run-of-the-mill dinner party, but a classy gathering of sophisticated thinkers. We would all sit at full attention, hanging on her every word. Plus, she's the only person I can think of who could succeed in getting the conversation back on track after Kathie Lee traipsed through the room wearing nothing but a lampshade on her head.

Beyoncé

You know I loves me some Beyoncé, and if I invited Gaga, I'd have to invite Queen Bey or she'd be jealous! With her voice like butter and her skin like caramel, I'd be tempted to ask Richard Simmons for permission to even give her a hug. She's so bootylicious, I'd put a ring on it! That's why no dinner party of mine, fantasy or otherwise, would be complete without this talented triple threat. As I explained to Gaga, it's a casual event, so Beyoncé should leave her alter ego, Sasha Fierce, at home and come au naturel. I also love that Beyoncé always keeps it real and isn't afraid of her curves. Unlike most prissy pop stars who would turn their noses up and inquire "Is there dairy in this?" you know the only question Beyoncé would ask is "Hey, are there more of these slammin' lemon bars?" I, for one, am so ready for that jelly!

Hey, Martha, quick question. Has Beyoncé ever come to one of your dinner parties? No? Okay, just checking.

Meryl Streep

I couldn't possibly have a fantasy dinner party and not invite America's Best Actress EVER, the one and only Ms. Meryl Motherfuckin' Streep! Now, I would never make Meryl "sing for her supper," but I would have no problem subtly forcing her to "act for her appetizers." That's right. I would simply refuse to serve her anything unless she asked for it each time as a different character from her impressive list of screen credits.

"Ross," she'd ask. "May I have one of those delicious-looking baby back ribs?"

"Meryl, you know the rules," I'd respond. "Say it like that Australian lady you played in *A Cry in the Dark*."

She'd flatly refuse and defiantly cross her arms.

"Well, then, Meryl, I'm afraid the answer is no, you may not. You see, a dingo ate your baby back ribs."

Eventually, she'd get so ravenously hungry that she'd begrudgingly bust out an impromptu one-woman show featuring monologues by every character she'd ever played, all for a single popcorn shrimp. But this multiple Oscar-winning actress deserves much more than that, so I'd happily pile Meryl's plate high with whatever she wanted—a deal's a deal.

Howard Stern

It may surprise you that a mild-mannered Goody Two-shoes like myself is a super-fan of the undisputed King of All Media. You've got to love a guy who has said and done things so offensive, he's not only reportedly accumulated millions of dollars' worth of fines from the FCC but he carries them as a badge of honor. And rightfully so! Howard is fearless and brutally honest in the face of an increasingly bland status quo. Other guests like Meryl may be above a good fart joke, but I love 'em and Howard can deliver one better than anybody. That skill *alone* is worth an invitation! He possesses that rare combination of chutzpah, heart, and brains, all in equal amounts. I simply adore him and I know in my gut that he'd lend an unsettling but much needed element of danger to my gathering. The moment people walk in and see Howard, they'll know that, at this dinner party, anything goes! Plus, he's a genius conversationalist at social gatherings—he can talk about everything from Transcendental Meditation to lesbian porn stars (if it weren't for him, I'd know nothing about either).

Oprah

If I'm going to invite the King of All Media to my party, then I must have the Queen, too! Just imagine all the scandalous and spirit-lifting stories we'd hear from Lady O (that's what I'd call her)! We'd all choke on our arugula and goat cheese as she spilled the dirt on Tom Cruise. And we'd gasp in shock as she coyly discussed when Celebrity X flirted with her during commercial breaks. I'll never tell who—my discretion is one of the reasons Lady O and I will be such close friends. (Okay, it was Tom Cruise. Dammit! I did it *again*!)

I don't know if you notice a pattern here, but even people I adore and revere are put to work at my dinner parties. Them's the rules in the Mathews household. So I'd have Oprah announce each course in her hallmark booming voice that she used on her TV show whenever she welcomed a guest or gave away a car. "IT'S TIME FOR ROAST BEEEEEEEEEEEEF WITH GRAAAAAAAAAVY!!! LOOK UNDER YOUR SEATS! *YOU* GET A ROLL AND *YOU* GET A ROLL AND *YOU* GET A ROLL..."

Shirley Phelps-Roper

The name doesn't ring a bell? Consider yourself lucky. If you have the displeasure of being aware of her, you know that she's the daughter of Fred Phelps, Sr.—the founder of the Westboro Baptist "Church"—and the very confused individual responsible for those repulsive "GOD HATES FAGS" signs used to disrupt and protest everything from AIDS Walks to soldiers' funerals. What ridiculous, blind hatred. God doesn't hate anyone, dummy! Surely, Shirley, you must be joking.

No matter how I try, I just can't fathom where Shirley's self-righteous, all-consuming anger comes from. My best guess to explain her unnatural across-the-board rage is that she's most likely never had a truly fabulous time at a truly fabulous dinner party with truly fabulous people. Perhaps she just needs a little love, laughter, and a delicious lemon bar or two? I'd cherish an opportunity to show this poor, misguided soul that she's not only completely wrong and spitting in God's face by spewing such dreadful hatred but she's missing out on one of the most important parts of life: FUN! I mean, do you think God put us on this Earth to stand around in ill-fitting clothes with unflattering haircuts while holding ugly signs and verbally assaulting wonderful people? No way, José!

At my dinner party, Ms. Phelps would enjoy both a great meal and a generous portion of "food for thought!" And I would kindly ask her to leave her unfortunate picket sign along with the pile of coats and purses on the bed in the guest bedroom (facedown, please). I'm hoping that after a few hours with me and my fabulous friends, she won't be needing it anymore.

• • • •

So now that the guest list is complete, let the party begin!

As everyone arrived, shirtless hunks would "work the room" with cute little trays of tempting finger foods. If there's one thing I've learned over the years, it's that everyone—from valet parking attendants to heads of state—just adores appetizers! I mean, what's not to love about mini egg rolls, stuffed mushroom caps, canapés, and Bunka's delicious little Swedish meatballs that you can easily pop right into your mouth while making small talk? And how about those hunky servers, huh? Hey, Kathie Lee, please only grab the balls on the serving tray! Thanks!

The great thing about hors d'oeuvres (which is spelled so weird and always looks to me like "horse ovaries"—the last thing I'd ever want to see on the end of a toothpick) is that they're perfect for everyone, regardless of which end of the spectrum their eating disorder happens to fall. Think about it—the food-phobic "skinny minnies" can take one measly steamed veggie dumpling off the tray and pretend to nibble at it all night, while the snack-scarfin' Sasquatches on the other side of the room can eat dozens of deep-fried cream-cheese-and-crabmeat wontons without being judged. I mean, it's not like anyone's keeping count, right? When they're gone, they're gone. And who needs appetizers anyway? It's time for dinner!

I would invite everyone to dig and, oh, how they would! Leftovers, schmeftovers! Like a proud papa, I'd sit back and take a moment to soak in the evening and admire my handiwork. As I scanned the room, I would notice the various groupings of my guests.

Shirley Phelps would be busy chatting with my mother while

Bunka gave Lady Gaga makeup tips: "Tone it down. You're a pretty girl!"

Rachel and Howard would be arm-wrestling for the last crescent roll, unaware that Meryl had just cruelly snatched it away while in character as Miranda Priestly, the icy fashion editor she played in *The Devil Wears Prada*. Kathie Lee, having finally sobered up, would be in the kitchen doing the dishes while Richard dried them with a sequined dish towel. And me? I'd be so immersed in everyone else, I'd barely even notice the strong hands of Justin Timberlake massaging my shoulders. What a guy.

"Justin," I'd whisper.

"Yeah, baby?"

"Have you ever massaged Martha Stewart?"

He'd pause for a moment. "Nope."

That's fucking right, you haven't.

Of course, after coffee and dessert (not a single lemon bar left!), the party would end like all great get-togethers do: with everyone gathered around the white baby grand, loudly singing along with Lady Gaga as she and I performed a duet of "Born This Way."

As I looked around the room at all my famous, brilliant and gorgeous friends, I would notice two things. First, singing louder than anyone else, really "selling it," would be—you guessed it—none other than Shirley Phelps. "I'm on the right track baby," she'd croon with her arm around Rachel's shoulder. "I was born this way!"

Hmmm, I guess she really won't be needing that sign anymore, huh?

And second, Kathie Lee would be making out with Justin. And you know what? More power to her! Because just like in Vegas, what happens at Ross's Fantasy Celebrity Dinner Party *stays* at Ross's Fantasy Celebrity Dinner Party. That is, except for Shirley's horrible sign. It's garbage now, but as a passionate recycler, I'd like to think I could come up with an idea for a fantastic art project to turn that sign into something both fabulous and functional. Something like a cute little planter for my herb garden or a gorgeous Chinese lantern. And I'd know exactly where to go for the step-by-step instructions for the project: MarthaStewart.com. Because, let's face it—if anyone could transform something as ugly as that sign into something beautiful, it would be Martha. Dammit, even in my fantasies, I've got to admit it—she really is the best.

QUIZ

Are You a Name Dropper?

By this point in the book, you know what a name dropper is, you know what a name dropper does, and you know what a name dropper looks like. Well, now it's time for you, dear reader, to take a good, long look in the mirror and ask yourself a very important question: Are you a name dropper?

Of course, I don't expect you to answer this monumental question on your own. That kind of self-reflection takes years of intense psychotherapy and, to be quite frank, I don't have time for that—I'm a very busy man. So, to help you quickly determine whether or not you're a bona fide name dropper, I've created a simple, easy-to-take quiz.

Warning: This test is unscientific, totally frivolous, and an absolute waste of time.

So let's begin!

Before we start, I'd like to go over a few rules. First, don't be ashamed—being a name dropper isn't a bad thing. It just means that you care! Second, make sure you answer honestly—I'll know if you're lying. (Ever since that time I forgot to unplug my crockpot before washing it and got shocked like a mofo, I've been picking up on some serious psychic energy.) And last, I want to know your results! So, after you take the quiz, tweet me your results @HelloRoss.

Get it? Got it? Good. Let's go!

1. You're attending a big Hollywood red carpet movie premiere. You're dressed to the nines and looking like a total ten, but you have to go *number one*. You duck into the closest gender-neutral bathroom to relieve yourself before the movie starts. As you make your way to the nearest Tinseltown toilette, you hear a flush, see the star of the movie emerge from a stall, and exit the bathroom WITHOUT washing their hands. What do you do?

   a. Ignore it, but make a mental note NOT to shake their hand at the after-party.

   b. Immediately post a tweet that doesn't name names, but gives not-so-subtle hints as to who they are and what they did.

   c. Follow the star out of the bathroom while yelling at the top of your lungs, "WASH YOUR HANDS, LADY! JUDI DENCH?!? MORE LIKE DOODY STENCH!"

2. You run inside a coffee shop, rushing to get caffeinated before a big meeting. When you get inside, you're shocked at how long the line is. Suddenly, the person in front of you senses your desperation and politely lets you cut in front of them in

line. As you leave with your nonfat Grande Caffe Americano you turn to see that your Good Samaritan was, in fact, nonfat American treasure Ariana Grande. What do you do?

a. Smile and silently mouth the words, "Thank u, next."

b. Frantically reach for the cell phone in your pocket to take a selfie, but spill scalding hot coffee all over yourself in the process.

c. Screw your important meeting. Stay in line, buy Ariana Grande a Venti coffee and SnapChat your conversation as you try to convince her that she really needs a new hairdo—that high-pony look is dunzo, girl!

3. You're at the drug store to pick up a few personal items and you spot your favorite male pop star buying extra-small condoms, genital wart cream, and a family-size bag of Cool Ranch Doritos. What do you do?

a. Pretend you don't even recognize him and give him his space. After all, size doesn't really matter (of course I'm talking about the family-size bag of Doritos).

b. Say hello and be supportive! Offer him your twenty-percent-off coupon for genital wart cream. After all, you have plenty left at home anyway (coupons, not cream).

c. Snap a pic of everything in his basket and post it on your Instagram with #BabyDick.

4. You're at the local Hollywood dog park and you're mortified when another pooch starts mercilessly humping your dog. Just then, the other dog's owner runs over to help separate his horny hound from your dirty dog and you realize it's the star of your newest Netflix obsession. As he attempts to cock-block his cocker spaniel, what do you do?

    a. You're all bark and no bite, so you throw him a bone by pretending you don't even know who he is and it doesn't matter in the slightest that his dog just made your dog his bitch.

    b. Really unleash on him and rub his nose in it, while telling him that your K-9 isn't interested in 69'ing, doggone it!

    c. Let the dogs have at it, hoping that your dog gets pregnant. If they have puppies, you can file a paw-ternity suit for pup support! Ca-ching!

5. You're on a hookup app and you decide to meet up with a guy who has a pictureless profile and some pretty freaky fetishes. When your trick comes to the door, it turns out he's one of your favorite YouTubers. What do you do?

    a. Slam the door on the whore!

    b. Who cares? You take out your tube and play with the YouTuber's tube, too.

    c. Ask him to come back in five minutes, hide a camera in your bedroom, and broadcast your filthy fetish freak show fun on Facebook Live.

Okay, now it's time for your results!

Did you answer mostly As? Then you're an AMATEUR NAME DROPPER. Oh, honey, bless your sweet heart, but you won't be sittin' next to me at happy hour any time soon. It's not that I don't want you there, it's just that you're not ready for it yet. You could get hurt. Name dropping isn't a hobby—it's a way of life.

Did you answer mostly Bs? Then you're a PROFESSIONAL NAME DROPPER. You're not above making the most of a celebrity sighting, but you're also not quite yet a black belt in broadcasting your bump-ins with beloved bigwigs. May I suggest a bullhorn?

Did you answer mostly Cs? Oh wow! Congratulations! You're what is known as a MASTER NAME DROPPER. You stand proudly atop Mount Name Drop, having reached the ultimate pinnacle. I'm simultaneously impressed *and* scared to meet you. Really, you should probably think about getting a life. I should know. I'm a MASTER NAME DROPPER, too. I'd recommend that you write a book all about it, but . . . um, I just did.

THANK-YOUS

The idea for this book came to me when I was nude. I was in the shower, loofa'ing my gorgeous naked body, thinking about what I wanted to put out into the world. I had been asked recently, "Are you ever going to write another book?"

I honestly didn't know how to answer. If I did, what would it be? The question hounded me for months. But then, on that random morning in the shower as I was slathered in soapy suds, it hit me: just tell everybody the stories you tell your friends.

It was simple, really. I consider every fan I meet in an airport or a mall or at happy hour a friend right away, anyway. I've always felt that way. So I turned off the shower and walked across the bathroom to grab my phone. Dripping water all over the floor, I typed out ideas for thirteen chapters. And now here they are, for all to see.

Writing a book is a scary process. The idea, it turns out, is the easy part. Actually writing it is daunting and scary—like opening up your soul and inviting strangers in. But I am so grateful to be sharing these stories with you. So before I thank anyone, I want to thank you for spending your hard-earned money on this book.

I hope it helped us become better friends, and most important, I hope it made you laugh.

Next, I have to thank two people who I love to create with and who helped me tremendously with this book. First, the incredibly talented and hilarious drag icon Jackie Beat, who was by my side (or on the phone) for nearly every word of *Name Drop*. Thanks for always making work seem like play. And second, my bestie since high school and the extraordinary writer and producer Taya Faber. Thank you for always making everything better.

A big thanks to my podcast family, Nikki Boyer, Chris "CJay" Jordan, Fagsy Malone, Trish Suhr, and Josh "JRod" Rodriguez. They have been so supportive throughout the writing process, never throwing a fit when I needed to reschedule a recording.

I'm so grateful for my strong team, starting with my manager of more than a decade, Mark Degenkolb. I give you a lot of shit, but you're very good at what you do. I'm so thankful to my assistant Trisha, who takes such good care of my life. Also, thanks to my lawyer Steve Warren, my literary agent Brandi Bowles at UTA for her priceless guidance and for introducing me to my editor Rakesh Satyal at Simon & Schuster. Rakesh, this process with you was a joy. Thank you for trusting my vision and for not being mad when I missed my deadline . . . more than once.

When I was a kid, I used to read the *Little House on the Prairie* books every night before I went to bed. I think my mom probably found the set of used books at a garage sale or thrift store. They were old, worn, and smelled musty. I loved them. At the beginning of every chapter, there was an illustration of what was about to occur. I remember being so tired one night, but seeing a drawing of Laura falling into the creek and thinking, *Well now I have to read the next chapter!*

That's why I wanted *Name Drop* to have illustrations—to make you curious about what stories the next page would tell. So a huge thanks to Brad Gibson, who made the fantastic illustrations for this book. Brad is a listener of my podcast *Straight Talk* and I love his work. Well done, Brad.

And, of course I have to thank my *RuPaul's Drag Race* family, including the legend herself, RuPaul. Ru—I'll never be able to adequately express my gratitude for allowing me to sit next to you. And thank you to my cojudges and (more importantly) close friends, Michelle Visage and Carson Kressley. I love you both dearly. And thank you to the all the producers and talented people at World of Wonder and VH1 who make *RuPaul's Drag Race* a global phenomenon. I am so honored and happy to be on your team.

There are so many other important people to thank, and I'm sure I'm missing a ton. My family—my dad, my mom's husband Don Huddleston, brother Eric, nephew Kai, aunts, uncles, cousins, and Bunka. Icons who have supported me like Jay Leno, Chelsea Handler, and Rosie O'Donnell. My former partner and dear friend Salvador Camarena. The fabulous people of my favorite place on Earth, Palm Springs. My beloved, loyal Straight Talkers. Friends—Boni Killion, Scott Atwell, Arleen Cohen, Daria Benedict, Molly Landreth, Dr. Neighbor, Sista Neighbor, Bethie Hungerford, Sean Maley, David Hasslinger, Adan Villalobos, Sammy Miclette, Tommy Fields, Anthony Caleca, Jessie Gaskell, Marissa Jaret Winokur, Diana Degenkolb, Amy Vorhees, Bill "The Gay Senior Citizen Movie Critic" Golian, the entire Camarena family, and so many others.

And a special thank-you to Ryan Fogarty, who encouraged me to focus on this book, made me feel like I could actually write it, and created two beautiful spaces for me to create.

Extra cuddles and kisses to my doggies, Audrey, Selena, and Pa Earl, and to my angels in heaven, Louise and Mijo. Daddy loves you all so much.

Finally, I have to thank my mom—a woman who raised me to believe that I could accomplish anything. During the writing of this book, she fought and beat breast cancer like the champion she is. But then it came back. When I was a little boy and got scared, my mom would kiss my palm, close my hand, and say, "Open this up whenever you need a kiss."

I'm still holding that kiss tight.

My mom is the biggest, best, and most impressive name I could ever drop. I love you.

Until book number three, Mathews out.

ABOUT THE AUTHOR

Ross Mathews is one of the most in-demand television personalities and pop culture experts in entertainment today. He is a judge on the Emmy Award–winning show *RuPaul's Drag Race*, the bestselling author of *Man Up!: Tales of My Delusional Self-Confidence*, and the host of the weekly pop culture podcast, "Straight Talk with Ross Mathews." He lives in Los Angeles and Palm Springs.

National Bestseller!

Ross Mathews's laugh-out-loud and inspiring journey as a super-fan, from his atypical childhood to his loud, proud, unapologetically genuine self on national television.

Available in paperback, ebook, and audio